I WANT SOME TOO

A LIFE-CHANGING LOOK AT PAUL'S LETTER TO THE CHURCH IN EPHESUS

Advantage
BOOKS

Dr. John R. Adolph

This book is dedicated to:

Jesus Christ and His finished work on the cross.

To devout believers in the Lord whose human insufficiency, flawed humanity and personal inadequacy demand and necessitates the cross of Christ and the grace of God.

To sincere followers of Jesus Christ who are guilty of trying to "stick to the rules" for God to love you and have failed miserably.

To active Sunday morning worshippers who, at times look down their noses at people who are not quite like they are in the general assembly of the saints because they are evident sinners looking for a God who will give them another chance.

To in-active church members around the world who "used to be" actively involved in church but have fallen by the wayside because of the overwhelming noticeable sins of church folks.

To legalistic Pastors who paint themselves in the light of human perfection instead of the precious reality of the Lord's redemption.

To hypocritical church leaders who would dare point the finger at the errors of others while missing the sins they face each day when they look at the sinner in the mirror.

To religious elitist that have sought to downplay the virtue and value of God's grace while at the same time elevating the supposed good news of human works.

To wayward sinners who find no hope in the church because you just do not fit in.

To every real Christian that can openly admit that without God's grace you would be nothing.

Table Of Contents

John R. Adolph

ACKNOWLEDGEMENTS

Once while the great church reformationist, Martin Luther was in silent confession to God regarding his known sins, he stayed before the Lord an interminable period. When he was asked what took him so long, he replied by saying, "every time I thought I was finished I discovered another sin I needed to confess." I dare not speak for you, but I want to be transparent as I pen the words of this text and say openly that I know what Martin Luther felt like. There have been times I have wanted to walk away from the faith because no matter how hard I have tried I just never seem to be able to get it all right. Wait, do not misconstrue my sincere and devout love for Jesus Christ who is my Lord, King, Savior, and God. I love Him with everything that I have in me. When I pause to look closely at what I am, there are days that I dislike what I see. Have you ever been there before? Have you ever paused as a Christian to give in-depth consideration to your human weaknesses, personal flaws and hang-ups that you wish you could do away with?

A few years ago I embarked on a study of the book of Ephesians, and it transformed my life forever. Paul's view of grace made me understand why it is something that none of us could afford to live without. At the time of my study, I did not have a book like this in mind. What I had in mind at the time was feeding the flock of Antioch Missionary Baptist Church in Beaumont, Texas a solid diet of doctrinally sound Biblical truth that would honor God and strengthen His people. I was also covertly hoping to discover some answers to some of my hard to answer questions like "why am I like I am?" As I studied this Pauline masterpiece, I saw something that I had heard about all of my life but had somehow missed. I saw and came in touch with grace!

The root of my study of Paul's letter to the church at Ephesus has become the fruit of this work. I cannot help but say "thank you" to Dr. David Rensberger and Dr. Wayne Merritt of the Interdenominational Theological Center in Atlanta, Georgia for their critical study of the Greek New Testament that involves the book of Ephesians. I must also thank

Dr. Edward P. Wimberly for his use of story as it relates to divine expressions of grace ever present in our daily human reality. Most importantly, I am forever indebted to the flock that I feed week in and week out. I know that every sermon and lesson that I have taught over the years have not been a masterpiece. However, it is my sincere hope that they have been thin enough in human reason that the grace of the cross could be seen.

Moreover, I pray that the lessons I have preached both with my lips and my life of service to God have been filled with enough of God's grace that it compels you to serve the Lord until time is no more.

INTRODUCTION

The bitter chill of a rather icy winter was slowly starting to fade, and the warmth of spring was on the horizon. I found myself in deep thought regarding the true message of the cross and the true meaning of grace. Initially, I found the subject matter of grace simple enough for an infant to tread across its magnificent width safely, but its depth was so far beneath what my mind could ponder I knew I could never touch its bottom. In my mind's eye, the crossbeam of grace was wide enough to fit the "whosoever will" onto it comfortably. Its height, tall enough to kiss the cheek of God and cause Him to grant mercy to sinners like me; and its bottom deep enough to touch the heated billows of a burning hell with love so real that no one would want to spend the night there let alone an eternity. As I prepared to feed the flock of God at the Antioch Church, I felt pushed and pressed to devote my study to Paul's letter to the church at Ephesus. As soon as I began studying this great epistle, I understood why. It is a letter about grace!

On one occasion I stopped to converse with a very dear friend of mine, Dr. Delbert Mack from the Cathedral of Faith Church in Beaumont and he asked me what I was studying, and I responded with great joy, "the book of Ephesians!" He then said, "Adolph, you have to get the commentaries on that letter written by Dr. D. Martin Lloyd Jones." Mack suggested it, I did it, and I have never regretted it. One of the most profound comments Dr. Jones makes is that when Paul says, ***"Grace be to you and peace from God our Father and the Lord Jesus Christ"*** (1:2, KJV) that it was his entire letter written in one sentence. The rest of the letter is his explanation of what that one verse contained. Wow! If the argument of Dr. Jones is true, grace then becomes the thematic discourse of this entire epistle. It runs through the letter like a crimson chord through a beautiful white quilt. Grace presented, grace extended, grace maintained, grace that directs and grace that protects.

Grace. What a marvelous word. Grace. What a divine concept. Grace. What a life changing, mind-altering, soul saving reality. Grace! It is what this work is all about. Please understand, this book is not a systematic treatise on grace, neither is it a commentary on the book of Ephesians, though it does contain numerous comments. It is not an exegetical reprise on Paul's work, though it does, without a doubt provide exegesis. This book is not just a devotional book filled with prayers, meditative and contemplative thought, though it too contains all of the aforementioned. This book is a journey through

Paul's letter that makes the grace of God something that you cannot afford to live without.

This book is a journey through the letter of Ephesians. The emphasis and impetus of this work is to get each reader to spend just seven minutes a day reading, hearing, listening, and encountering the words of the Apostle Paul as he enlightens and empowers us through the person of the Holy Ghost. Each chapter of this book will contain four significant shifts: the truth about grace, the treasure of His goodness, the triumph that He gives and a short talk with God, respectively. Each movement in the chapter is designed to deepen and broaden what has been printed in the sacred text that is being used.

FOR ENHANCED EBOOK READERS AND DVD VIEWERS

If you are reading this book as an enhanced eBook a video has been provided, a short movie of sorts. This feature has been added so that the pages of the printed text of Ephesians can take on a modern-day pulse. When you arrive at the video link simply open it and watch the letter of Ephesians unfold like a drama on a Tinseltown screen. If you are using a DVD simply place it in your viewing device and press play. You will meet fascinating characters; encounter church dilemmas and moments of laughter and healing as you watch. Once the video clip concludes, take a moment and consider the devotional questions that are listed in the section labeled "from the director's chair." The questions posed should make reading Ephesians exciting and learning its principles life transforming at best.

When all is said and concluded, this book is designed to paint the grace that Paul presents to the Ephesian Church in such a way that you will say, if this grace is true *I WANT SOME TOO!*

Chapter 1

Don't Panic,
He's Got A Plan!

Week 1
<u>The Grace Of The Trinity</u>

Day 1-Week 1
The Truth About Grace

I had been flushing the paper towels down the toilet. I knew that I was supposed to be throwing them in the waste paper basket, but at home, it just seemed easier to flush them to me. So flush them I did. How many did I flush? Let's just say I had flushed them on numerous occasions, but after you do the wrong thing enough times you lose count right? One day my dad came home with Houston Astros baseball tickets. I was so excited! He told my younger brother Ron and me to get dressed. I dashed to the closet to find my sneakers and Astros baseball jersey and Ron rushed to get cleaned up in the bathroom. Just then I heard the most disturbing cry ever. My brother yelled for help because the bathroom toilet was flooding the hallway. I thought to myself how could this be?

I'm not a plumber but I had seen enough Roto-Rooter commercials to know a thing or two, so I grabbed the plunger and went into action. Water is now covering the hallway and up pops a clot of paper towels! Ron says, "Ooooooh how did these get in there?" To which I replied, "All of us use paper towels so we will never know. Let's just get the water up." The plunger wasn't working and the toilet was giving us all of the water it had in it plus some.

My dad heard the commotion and said, "What in the world is going on?" I looked up and confessed. I told my dad I had been putting the paper towels in the toilet. He put his hand on his hip, grinned sheepishly and said, "I'll be right back." I thought our game in the Astrodome was over. Ron looked at me and said, "Don't panic, he's got a plan!" Just then my dad walked into the bathroom with a contraption that looked like something Spider-Man would use. He poked it down the commode as far as it could go and pulled it out. It came up with all of my paper towels attached! My father then said, "I knew you would do this, so I was prepared for it!" Without any judgment towards me, he said with a smile on his face "Let's go watch the Astros beat the Braves!"

No Christian no matter how holy, sacred, sincere, or devout they are will get it all right. In short, there are no perfect people. NONE! In fact, God knew that we would make a mess of it all, so He fostered a plan that is mind-blowing. He sat down and had a meeting with Himself and decided to become one of us to save all of us who would dare to believe! It is the work of a triune God, and it is completely grace-driven.

God knew that you would need a Savior, so He became one. God knew that you would need cleansing, so He died just for you. God knew that you would need sustaining so He provided you with His spirit. He knew that you would fall flat on your face so He provided even more grace so that you could never fall too far away from Him to save you!

Here is the truth about grace, God knew about the mess you would get yourself into, but He already had a plan to save you from the consequences.

The Treasure Of His Goodness

Paul, an apostle of Jesus Christ by the will of God, to the saints which are at Ephesus, and to the faithful in Christ Jesus: Grace be to you, and peace, from God our Father, and from the Lord Jesus Christ (1:1-2, KJV).

You are now starting to read an Epistle of the New Testament. It is simply a letter written from one person to another. In this case, this is a letter written from Paul to the Church of God located in the seaport town of Ephesus.

The Paul of this letter is also the Saul of Tarsus. Saul is Paul before conversion and Paul is Saul after he met Jesus Christ. With this in mind, every believer should have a story to tell regarding the change Jesus Christ has made in his or her life. For Paul, he went from persecuting the church of God to preaching the Gospel of Jesus Christ and telling the world he lived in about God's grace.

Paul declares openly that he is an "Apostle...by the will of God." What he is celebrating here is the fact that he did not choose God and ask to serve. God chose him and commanded that he preach. In short, God does not call Paul because he is qualified; He calls Paul because Paul is God's choice. Here is some exciting news for you. There are some things in your past that should disqualify you from service to God based on the standards of others. But what disqualifies you in the minds of people qualifies you in the heart of God.

This letter is written from Paul to the "saints" who are located in the city of Ephesus. In our current culture, saints are considered to be dead. But, that is not biblically true. Saints are sinners that have been saved by grace and are faithful in Christ. Keep this in mind; you are not a saint because you are dead, you are a saint because you are alive in Jesus Christ.

The best news of these two verses is that Paul extends to the church the grace of the Lord Jesus. In short, Jesus is not just some ordinary guy. He is Lord! This means He is in control. Moreover, if Paul could give you a gift right now, it would not be a car, a house, good health or fame. He would give you grace! The Greek word for grace used here is *charis.* It means God's unmerited favor. Notice that peace comes along with it. The Greek word for peace used here is ***iraynay.*** It is has nothing to do with the absence of chaos as much as it does the presence of God. Here is how it works. Wherever you find God's grace deposited, you will always have His peace produced. You cannot have one without the other.

The Triumph That He Gives

- Have you ever made the same mistake over and over and over again? How did it make you feel?

- What is the most significant struggle that you have as a Christian? Be radically honest with yourself for a moment. What makes this area a struggle for you? Is it your flesh? Your fear? Your faithlessness? What is it?

- What if you learned right now that God knew that this would be a struggle for you? How would you feel?

- What if God not only knew that this area of life would be a struggle for you but had a plan to deliver you and set you free in Jesus Christ? Would you accept it?

- People often want grace and need peace. What if you could have grace and peace right now?

A Short Talk With God

Lord Jesus Christ thank you for your grace! Without it, life is not worth living. Your grace makes each day of my life get sweeter and sweeter. I admit that my life is not all it should be. But, as of right now I say yes to your plan for me. Use the mistakes of my past as a witness for your grace in the present. Take what some would say should disqualify me and qualify me by way of your grace. Use my life for your glory. In the name of Jesus, I pray. Amen!

FROM THE DIRECTORS CHAIR

Click or type this link into your browser to view: https://youtu.be/ytftctz_AaA

1. What does an abundant life indeed consist of? Is money the only thing that matters? What really matters to you?

2. Ms. Dionese Ephraim is the main character in this film. What do you think about her so far?

3. Who do you think is running Dionese's life? Who do you think is really running your life?

4. What's stopping you from giving all of your life to God?

5. If you have surrendered, what do you feel God wants from you now?

Day 2-Week 1
The Truth About Grace

The other day I was rushing away from the gym and saw a small huddle of men gathered around the television. I just knew it was a game they were watching, so I just walked briskly through the small crowd. A young man grabbed me by the elbow and said: "Pastor what are you doing, where are you going?" I said, "I'm on my way to an evening meeting." He then whispered and said, "Dude no one walks when this show is on. It's disrespectful" (as he blushed at me). I paused to peep at the screen, and it was a game show! They were all watching "Who Wants To Be A Millionaire!" From that moment I fell in love with the game.

The reason I love it is because as believers in Christ we have access to much more than a million dollars could ever afford to buy us. And, we have a lifeline partner whose name is Jesus Christ who will never let us down. In fact, He's not just smart, He knows it all. Literally!

So I have invented my own game show, and it is called "Who Wants To Me More Than A Millionaire?" My game does not come with a laundry list of questions, just two or three to be exact. Want to play? Who woke you up this morning? Who died for your sins? Who arose three days later? Who has kept you all of your life? Who has blessed you above and beyond measure? For more than a million, your answer should have been Jesus Christ, Son of the living God.

Here is the truth about grace; to have Jesus Christ is to have it all!

The Treasure Of His Goodness

Blessed be the God and Father of our Lord Jesus Christ, who hath blessed us with all spiritual blessings in heavenly places in Christ (1:3, KJV).

1. There are only twenty-four words written in this one small verse and "blessed, " or its derivative is written at least three times. They are as follows: blessed, blessed and blessings. In short, when Paul writes the church at Ephesus he wants them to know that they are blessed, blessed, blessed.

2. The first word "blessed" means that you are blessed not because of what you have, but because of the God who has you.

3. The second word "blessed" defines those who have benefited from the Lord's goodness in any way, shape or fashion. In short, this word describes you. It says God has blessed you; God has kept you, God has provided for you and God will keep on taking care of you. In fact, God's beneficent behavior has benefited you all of your life.

4. The third word "blessings" describes the benefits of knowing Jesus Christ as Lord and Savior.

5. Notice these blessings are in "…heavenly places in Christ." This does not mean that you have to wait to die before you get these benefits even though there are blessings that we will receive in glory. It really says that the source of every earthly blessing has its roots in heavenly places. In short, all good and perfect gifts come from the Lord (James 1:17), and when we get them on earth, the source of that blessing is and will remain heaven.

The Triumph That He Gives

- How often do you worry about things instead of realizing that if God blessed you before with what you have needed, He could bless you again?

- What role does grace play in your life each day?

- If you could put a dollar amount on all of the things God has blessed you with how much would it be? This may seem really silly but try. Think of all of the things that God has provided for you that money cannot buy. Consider all of the things that checks cannot write.

- Now consider this, God blessed you with all of those blessings and you did not deserve any of them. And, the even more significant news is this; God is not through blessing you yet. For the believer in Jesus Christ, there is still more to come!

- Remember this, to depend on Christ for everything is to love Him and not need anything.

A Short Talk With God

Lord, I realize that you have been more than good to me. You have been patient, loving, caring, forgiving, and kind. You have been sweeter than sweet. You have been there for me when no one else has and you have been my all in all. God, you are the one who blesses my soul with everything that I have and will ever need in life. Forgive me for worrying and doubting your provisions. Thank you for making sure that regardless of my circumstances I am always blessed, blessed, blessed! In the name of the one who makes me more than a millionaire, in the name of Jesus I pray. Amen!

Day 3-Week 1
The Truth About Grace

Driving in the city of Beaumont where I live can be a beautiful thing. We have seven exits, a few thousand people, and seven cars at a red light can be considered a traffic jam. However, driving in Dallas, Los Angeles, Atlanta, and Houston requires spiritual giftedness, extreme holiness, and a degree of sacredness that I just do not have. I mean to drive in Houston is to ride in traffic at all hours of the day. Not to mention that there is always an accident, always some construction going on and if it rains, that automatically means that there will be an ambulance on the scene, rubbernecking taking place and a delay that says you will have plenty of time to read billboard signs that you would usually miss while traveling sixty miles per hour.

It is Thursday, April 23, 2015, and traffic is demonically possessed on I-45 in Houston near the Woodlands. I finally make my way into the city after traveling an average of five miles per hour without the use of my gift of known tongues, and we stop again. Break lights go as far as the eye can see. It is a test of the evil one, and I refuse to let him win. So I began reading billboard signs. This one to my east grabs my attention and keeps it. It read, "Find Out Who The Father Is Dial 1-800 Who's Your Daddy." I was floored.

Paternity tests are taking place all over. You know the old saying, "It's momma's baby, but it's daddy's maybe?" Rarely do we ever think of such in regards to God. The reason for this is because we believe that all of us are God's children, but I beg to differ. All of us are God's creation, but not all of us are God's children! In order to be His child, you have to be genetically regenerated to be in the family. In short, you must be born-again (John 3:1-21).

Here is the truth about grace, if God were to administer a paternity test on you right now, you would not just be 99.99999999% His, you would be His 100%! In fact, you are His, and He is yours!

The Treasure Of His Goodness

According as he hath chosen us in him before the foundation of the world, that we should be holy and without blame before him in love: having predestinated us unto the adoption of children by Jesus Christ to himself, according to the good pleasure of his will, to the praise of the glory of his grace, wherein he hath made us accepted in the beloved (1:4-6, KJV).

1. The best news of the day is that God chose you to be one of His! I know you think that you chose Christ, but there is something more profound for you to consider. He chose you before the foundations of the world were ever established. This means you were not elected to your position; you were selected to be His child. Are you rejoicing yet? What are you waiting on? God wanted children, and He picked you to be one of His.

2. It is what the Bible calls adoption. The blessing of adoption is that the adopter chooses the children while they are unwanted wards of the state. Get this, if God had to chose a child to claim to be His and there was one child in three hundred million, He would prefer you!

3. In fact, according to this text, your Father wanted you to be His so badly that He did not wait until you were born to adopt you. He picked you before your earthly parents knew you (Jeremiah 1).

4. Do you hear this passage yet? It says that you are chosen, you are holy and without blame. It means you are predestined. And it says you are adopted! You have the right to call God, your Father (Romans 8:12-14).

5. Now here is the kicker. Why did God make Himself your Father? Why did He adopt you and make you be a part of His royal family? He did it for the "praise of the glory of His grace." He did it so that when people saw you, they would know what grace looked like!

The Triumph That He Gives

- Have you ever felt like nobody cared about you or that no one really wanted you?

- Where do you think that thought came from?

- The blessing of being a believer is that there is never a time when God does not want you. Even when you have been with pigs, smell like hogs, and have squandered everything that He has ever given you and have nothing to show for it, you are still His child (Luke 15:11-End).

- What does being God's child mean to you?

- What do you think it means to Him?

A Short Talk With God

Lord, thank you for adopting me and making me one of your own. Thank you for making my name your name and your possessions my possessions. Lord, I know that being your child comes with standards attached, so help me become the kind of child that you would smile upon and favor. And, Lord when people that are not yours look at me; help me to model grace in such a way that I can tell them my dad is still adopting children. In my Father's name, Jesus I pray, Amen!

Day 4-Week 1
The Truth About Grace

No one wants to go to court unless you are a lawyer making a ton of money in a lawsuit. Other than that, the courtroom is just not the place you want to be. I once attended a court preceding that was mind-blowing. Richard and Randy (names have been changed to protect their true identity) were two terrific guys. However, they were really different. Richard was just always into something that got him into trouble and Randy was angelically kind. Richard got high and committed a horrible crime. It was not his first offense. In fact, Richie was a three-time loser and was set to do at least twenty-five years of state time.

We get to court, and both brothers show up along with a host of friends and relatives praying that the judge would give Richard grace and not justice. But, such was not the case. The Judge gave Richard the maximum sentence of twenty-five years and demanded that he be taken into custody immediately. But something took place that shocked only those who could tell them apart. Randy took his no good brother's place! That's right. Richard committed the crime, but before coming to court, Randy told his good for nothing twin brother that he would go to jail for him if he would spend the next five years of his life working to make himself better. Richard agreed, and Randy was taken into custody.

Of course, Jesus is not our twin brother, but He did take our place! He took on the punishment that was designed for us that day at the cross.

Here is the truth about grace, God paid the price for you, and it was not cheap. In fact, it cost Him everything, and in His heart, you were worth it!

The Treasure Of His Goodness

In whom we have redemption through his blood, the forgiveness of sins, according to the riches of his grace; wherein he hath abounded toward us in all wisdom and prudence; having made known unto us the mystery of his will, according to his good pleasure which he hath purposed in himself: that in the dispensation of the fullness of times he might gather together in one all things in Christ, both which are in heaven, and which are on earth; even in him: in whom also we have obtained an inheritance, being predestinated according to the purpose of him who worketh all things after the counsel of his own will: that we should be to the praise of his glory, who first trusted in Christ (1:7-12, KJV).

1. Please notice that in verses 4-6 we have the work of the Father. However, in verses 7-12 we have the work of the Son. The Father orchestrates a plan of adoption for you and the Son pays the price that the adoption will cost. Therefore, verse 7 begins like this, "In whom we have redemption…"

2. The Greek word used for redemption is the term ***Apollotrosis***. It means to buy a slave at full price by becoming the ransom for the slave that has been purchased.

3. The shouting news for you as you spiritually inhale this passage is found in the fact that Jesus took your place and He paid it all. Consider the method of redemption used for your deliverance; it is ransom by way of substitution. Consider the manner of redemption used to save you; it was the blood of the Lamb, which is why He had to die on the cross. Consider the measure of redemption used to set you free; all of your sins, past, present, and future have been forgiven and the means of redemption is purely the grace of God.

4. Are you shouting yet? You should be and here is why. You win in the end and your victory comes to you not because of what you have done, but because of what Jesus has done for you that you could never have done for yourself. Your life is all about Him. Jesus made God's will known to us. Jesus purposed in His heart to do this for you. Jesus will gather all of us who loves Him when the time is right, and Jesus will grant you the inheritance that is coming to you!

5. The question you should be asking yourself right now is why? Why has the Lord done all of this for me? Get this; it is not because you pray every day. It is not because you read your Bible on a regular basis and it is not because you are profoundly spiritual or seriously religious. It is "…according to the riches of His grace…. so that we should be to the praise of His glory." God wants people to look at you and see His grace and give Him glory for what He has done for you.

The Triumph That He Gives

- Have you ever felt worthless? What made you feel like this?
- What goes through your mind when you hear the word substitute?
- When you consider all that Jesus Christ has done for you, what do you feel?
- Why did He do it?

- Never forget this, God the Father adopted you into His family before the earth had an axis to spin on. And, Jesus Christ, His only begotten Son, paid the price of the adoption by redeeming you.

A Short Talk With God

Lord Jesus, I owe you my life. The life I now live is really yours because you bought it. I owe you because you hold the deed to my eternal existence in your hands. Thank you for loving me enough to die so that I might live. Use me for your glory and make me model your grace every day of my life. In the name of Jesus who is Lord and Christ I pray. Amen!

Day 5-Week 1
The Truth About Grace

There are some mistakes that I have made in my past that I will never repeat as long as I live. Okay, the Bible says that confession is good for the soul so here it goes. I took a group of forty-six children to an amusement park with no help or supervision. Psychotic right? Yes, I know. I was running around trying to keep up with all of those kids and when the end of the day came, I felt like a man being released from a prison sentence where hard time and corporal punishment were both mandatory. I would have done better with being flogged in public. My mind was wrecked, my body was beyond fatigued, and my attitude was horrible; my patience was gone, my prayer life had ended and my blood pressure required immediate medication.

It was one of the worst days of my life. "Come back here; don't do that; sit down; stop that; little boy come here; and, little girl, please don't say that" were phrases that plagued my mind long after the day had come to a close. But I did do one thing right. I made every child that belonged to me wear a lime green t-shirt. That's right! All of mine were wearing lime. That way when it was time for me to leave I could spot them a mile away. You see, I stamped them all so that when it was time for my day to end and the day was over, I could leave the park with those who were mine.

Here is the truth about grace; God has marked you. No, you are not wearing a lime green T-Shirt, but you have been sealed with the person of the Holy Ghost!

The Treasure Of His Goodness

In whom ye also trusted, after that ye heard the word of truth, the gospel of your salvation: in whom also after that ye believed, ye were sealed with that Holy Spirit of promise, which is the earnest of our inheritance until the redemption of the purchased possession, unto the praise of his glory (1:13-14, KJV).

1. Please notice as we study chapter one that God the Father has adopted you, God the Son redeemed you and now you will see the work of God the Holy Ghost.

2. Here's what is so exciting, the spirit seals you eternally. It is essential to know, that the seal of the Spirit happens at the moment of belief in the message of the

Gospel. When you heard about how Jesus died for you and arose from the dead, you were sealed by the Spirit forever.

3. It is imperative for you to know that there is a considerable difference between the sealing of the Spirit and the filling of the Spirit. You are sealed (stamped) once and for all, but the Spirit fills you over and over again (Eph. 5:18).

4. Most importantly, you are the "...earnest of our inheritance..." In short, God deposited the Spirit into your life. It is like, God put you on lay-a-way knowing that He would one day return to receive you so that He could spend all of eternity with you.

5. Now you have to ask yourself the billion-dollar question. Why did God do this for you? Here is the answer, "...unto the praise of His glory." God did it so that He could get the glory for what His grace could produce!

The Triumph That He Gives

*   What is the difference between the sealing of the Spirit and the filling of the Spirit?

*   Do you feel like you are Spirit-filled most of the time? Why or Why not?

*   Remember this, the filling of the Spirit and the sealing of the Spirit does not equal a feeling you get from the Spirit. You may not feel it, but you have it as soon as you believe in Jesus Christ.

*   You are God's child and you have been marked and sealed by Him forever. How does that make you feel?

*   Hold on to this truth; you are adopted by the Father, redeemed by the Son and sealed by the Holy Ghost.

A Short Talk With God

God of grace and Lord of mercy thank you for filling me with your presence, making me one of your own, keeping me in your care, and sealing me with your spirit until the day of redemption. Lord Jesus when I consider all that you have done for me, I feel compelled to serve you in a significant way. Use my life as a light to let others know that there is one true and living God, whose name is Jesus Christ. Amen.

Day 6-Week 1
The Truth About Grace

The story was told of a little girl who was asked to pray in her vacation bible school class. At the end of each day, one student would be asked to give the closing prayer and on this particular day, this little girl was asked to pray for her group. She rose to her feet and told her whole class to bow their heads and close their eyes and said "Dear God, A, B, C, D, E, F, G, H, I, J, K, L, M, N, O, P, Q, R, S, T, U, V, W, X, Y and Z now I've said my ABC's thank you God for hearing me. In Jesus name, Amen!" The entire class just erupted into laughter. The teacher asked her why did she say her ABC's instead of saying a prayer. The little girl replied, "My grandmother told me that God knows everything and He can surely work it out. So I never waste time with all of those fancy words, I just give Jesus my alphabets and He works everything else out for me. It works, you should try it sometime!"

Have you reached a point in your life where you know that the Lord will work it out for you? For many Christians, this is just not the case yet. Have you realized that God really does answer prayer? When you come to grips with the life-changing reality, everything around you will shift for the greater.

Here is the truth about grace; God answers your prayers not because He has to, but because He wants to.

The Treasure Of His Goodness

Wherefore I also, after I heard of your faith in the Lord Jesus, and love unto all the saints, cease not to give thanks for you, making mention of you in my prayers; that the God of our Lord Jesus Christ, the Father of glory, may give unto you the spirit of wisdom and revelation in the knowledge of him: the eyes of your understanding being enlightened; that ye may know what is the hope of his calling, and what the riches of the glory of his inheritance in the saints, and what is the exceeding greatness of his power to us-ward who believe, according to the working of his mighty power, which he wrought in Christ, when he raised him from the dead, and set him at his own right hand in the heavenly places, far above all principality, and power, and might, and dominion, and every name that is named, not only in this world, but also in that which is to come: and hath put all things under his feet, and gave him to be the head over all things to the church, which is his body, the fullness of him that filleth all in all (1:15-23, KJV).

1. Intercession is the form of prayer used by a Christian who is praying for someone other than themselves. It comes from the Greek word ***entugchano*** and it means to bear the weight of another. From verse 15 all of the way to verse 23 Paul prays, but he is not praying for himself, he is praying for the church at Ephesus.

2. Be careful with asking people to pray for you. It is not always a good practice. This is because some people have no desire to see you blessed or benefit from God's love and mercy. However, if you have a genuine friend in the faith, nothing at all beats their intercession for you. How do you know when you have a true friend? A true friend loves you in spite of your faults, embraces you when you fail and celebrates your blessings and your successes like they achieved them personally. That's a friend.

3. Paul loves this church and the people that make her who she is and he prays. It should be noted that when he prays, he does not ask for material wealth, physical health or any form of earthly prosperity. Is it wrong to petition heaven for things like this? No. It's just that things of this world are always temporal and not eternal. Paul's heart for the people is much more on an eternal plain than it is an earthly place.

4. If Paul could pray for you what do you think he would ask God for? The answer to this question lies in the confines of this passage. Here is what Paul would ask God to do for you:

    *   He would ask God to give you a spirit of Wisdom and Revelation-By this he means that He would ask God to steer you. To give you clarity in what you do so that what you do, is what God wants to be done.

    *   He would ask God for your eyes to be Enlightened-The consequence of having wisdom and revelation is to have eyes that can see. Please note that Paul is speaking regarding spiritual foresight. This kind of sight is not what you see with your eyes, but what you perceive through faith with your soul.

    *   He would ask for your understanding to be increased-To know the will of God is one thing, but for God to give you understanding is an extra added benefit. Paul wants you to understand because it builds faith and confidence in the Lord like nothing else can.

- Finally, he wants you to know the hope of His calling and all that this hope brings with it-In short; Paul wants you to know Him. He wants you to know the riches of His glory, His exceeding great power, and the fullness of who Jesus Christ really is.

5. The word "know" that Paul uses in this passage comes from the Greek term ***ido*** and it means to know because you are related to someone. It is one thing to have God as a Father, but do you know Him? It is another thing to have Jesus as a redeemer, but how much do you know about Him? It is great to be sealed and filled with the Spirit, but how much about the person of the Holy Ghost do you really know? Paul's prayer says I want you to know Him!

The Triumph That He Gives

- Getting to know someone takes time. How much time do you honestly give God a day? Be honest.

- If you don't make time for God, He will make time for Himself. Has He ever done this to you? What happened?

- Remember this, to be in God's company causes you to become like the company you keep. Spend some quality time with God.

A Short Talk With God

"Dear God, A, B, C, D, E, F, G, H, I, J, K, L, M, N, O, P, Q, R, S, T, U, V, W, X, Y and Z now I've said my ABC's thank you God for hearing me. In Jesus name, Amen!"

Chapter 2

That's Not Who I Am, It's Who I Used To Be!

Week 2
The Grace Of Transformity

Day 1-Week 2
The Truth About Grace

Call me crazy, but there are times I ride around and read church billboard signs. Some of them are pretty good. Here are a few of them that grabbed my attention.

Honk If You Love Jesus
Text While Driving If You Want to Meet Him

Looking For A Life Guard?
Ours Walks On Water

God Does Not Believe In Atheists
Therefore Atheists Do Not Exist

Son Screen Prevents Sin Burn

The Fact That There's A Highway To Hell
And Only A Stairway To Heaven Says A Lot About
Anticipated Traffic Numbers

We Are Still Open Between Christmas And Easter

Choose The Bread Of Life Or You're Toast

What Happens In Vegas Is Forgiven Here

Satan Knows Your Name But Calls You By Your Sins
God Knows Your Sins But Calls You By Your Name

We Don't Change God's Message
His Message Changes Us

One Sunday I was walking into worship, and an usher opened the door to let people in. One guy came in with his pants nearly dragging the ground with a mouth full of gold plated teeth. When he got into the foyer he spoke to the usher at the door like this; he said, "O snap, what's up J-Dub!" To which the young man serving as an usher replied, "That's Not Who I Am, It's Who I Used To Be." His friend who was apparently a blast from his past said, "Who you used to be? Man, you look the same to me Dub" and then snickered. But the usher replied, "My name used to be J-Dub but just call me James. What has happened to me just might happen to you if you quit tripping and listen to the message."

Here's a great question to ask. Has the message changed you any? The real truth of the matter is this, all of us still have some of the old us in us, but when you have heard the message, it will not let you remain the same.

The truth about grace is this; the message of God's love changes us from the inside out and not just the outside in.

The Treasure Of His Goodness

And you hath he quickened, who were dead in trespasses and sins; wherein in time past ye walked according to the course of this world, according to the prince of the power of the air, the spirit that now worketh in the children of disobedience: among whom also we all had our conversation in times past in the lusts of our flesh, fulfilling the desires of the flesh and of the mind; and were by nature the children of wrath, even as others. But God, who is rich in mercy, for his great love wherewith he loved us, even when we were dead in sins, hath quickened us together with Christ, (by grace ye are saved;) and hath raised us up together, and made us sit together in heavenly places in Christ Jesus: that in the ages to come he might show the exceeding riches of his grace in his kindness toward us through Christ Jesus (2:1-7, KJV).

1. Please hear this; every real Christian should have a story of who they were before meeting Jesus Christ. If you do not have a story like this and you call yourself a Christian, it could very well mean that you are still what you used to be.

2. To put it bluntly, the grace of the Lord Jesus Christ transforms us. Paul describes it beautifully in this passage. First of all, there was a time that we were "...dead in trespasses and sins..." Retranslation, there was a time that you were living wrong and loving it. But, you discovered that it did not love you. During that time in your life, you did what the world did and was doing wrong even though you knew right. But God did not leave you in that condition!

3. You should be rejoicing right now and here is why. God never leaves you as He found you. Verse 4 says, "But God..." These two words imply and suggest that God is about to turn your entire life upside down so that He can set your life right side up.

4. Notice how God does this for you. The text says "...with His great love wherewith He loved us, even when we were dead in sins..." So here is how God delivers us from our sins and never forget it. He does not beat you, punish you or even give up on you. God does not wait for you to get it all right. What God does is so amazing it should bring tears to your eyes and joy to your heart. God is so merciful that He merely loves you while you are living wrong until you want to love Him back and learn to live right. This is the real message of the cross, and it is the core of the message of God's grace. Hold on to this truth; God loves you like crazy!

5. Here's our billion-dollar question again. Why does God love you so much? Here is why He loves you like He does, "...so that He might show the exceeding riches of His grace..." God says, "I've been putting up with your foolishness for years so that when I get through changing you, everyone will have to know just how wonderful my grace is."

The Triumph That He Gives

*   Do you remember when God changed your life?

*   What made you know that your change came from God?

- Have you made any huge mistakes since the time you gave your life to the Lord?

- Why do you think God did not give up on you and just throw you away after you failed and faltered?

- Remember this; God loves you more than you could fathom or imagine.

A Short Talk With God

Lord, I want you to know that you are the best thing that has ever happened to me. I have never understood a love like yours. Thank you for being patient with me, and I praise you for being the kind of God that would love me like I am until you mold me into what you want me to be. Forgive me for my mistakes and strengthen me so that I can conquer all of those things that seem to hold me back. I pray these petitions in the name of Jesus, Amen.

FROM THE DIRECTORS CHAIR

Click or type this link into your browser to view: https://youtu.be/70prCph2uQQ

1. Are there times when you feel that God has not changed your life at all?

2. There are times we make huge mistakes in life. Have you ever made at least one? How did you get over it?

3. Dionese is exceptionally prideful and she wants the Sinclair account. In what ways does pride affect your life?

4. There are times that we view success incorrectly. We tend to think that success is best seen in cars, clothes, cash, excellent credit scores and consumer products. However, after reading this chapter and viewing this clip, how would you now define success?

5. One of the great dangers for the Christian is to love things more than you love God. In what way is this happening to Dionese? Has it ever happened to you? How did you deal with it?

Day 2-Week 2
The Truth About Grace

Have you ever been so hungry you started seeing things? It happened to me once while in Seminary. The cafeteria was closed, none of my friends had any money, and I was broke and out of gas. I sat like a vagabond on the steps of my school with several of my friends as we dreamed of cheeseburgers and chicken wings. Just then, like a dream, a man walked into our administration building with a huge sandwich tray. Amazingly, none of us moved. We just sat there in disbelief until he said, "Hey you guys don't let all of that food go to waste it's free for you, but that tray was very expensive." We waited until he walked off and then jumped up like a group of savages and raced to the table and just started eating. We did not even bother to say our grace! We just ate. Chips, wings, sandwiches, croissants, cheese squares, salami, tuna, and roast beef. It was amazing. We belched without saying, "excuse me or pardon me." We ate without napkins, plates or utensils. We were hungry and hard-core.

About an hour later the tray was empty, and we were all full. We sat near the empty tray as if we had paid for it and we did not have one thin dime to our names. The same man that brought the tray returned to pick it up. He said, "This tray of food cost $249.00. It was free for you, but it cost the man that bought it big time." All I could think about at that moment was the cross and what the Lord had done for every Christian on that hill.

Here is the truth about grace, salvation might be free for us, but it cost the man that bought it big time!

The Treasure Of His Goodness

For by grace are ye saved through faith; and that not of yourselves: it is the gift of God: Not of works, lest any man should boast (2:8-9, KJV).

1. All too often church folks make being saved very difficult to understand. Some people will tell you that you have to dress a certain way, act a certain way and even do certain things. But please hear this, you are saved by grace alone, through faith alone, by Christ alone. Your salvation is a gift, and you do not pay for gifts, they are free.

2. This may sound foolish and simple, but when it comes to being saved, we often try to bargain with God. We attempt to embellish our lives by doing good so that we can abolish the moments, times and season when we have produced

things that are bad. This may prove to be very upsetting news to some, but you cannot do enough good to make God forget about your mistakes. Why? Our human sin is a matter of jurisprudence. Human sin is a matter of legal proportion. The law has been broken, and someone has to pay.

3. Now here is the question that makes God's grace so sweet. Who will pay for the crimes you have committed? Keep in mind; no lawyer on earth can represent you in heaven. God is the judge (He is the only one who is qualified to do so); Satan is the adversary and the accuser of the brethren (1 Tim. 4:13). His job is to bring the charges against you, and he will do a phenomenal job pleading his case for you to go to hell. You are a lawbreaker in the courtroom of eternal justice. What hope do you have? How can you get away from the punishment that fits the crimes you have committed against God? Here is what God's grace did just for you; God purchased a gift for you. It is like an insurance policy, only better. With insurance comes a premium that you have to work to pay for the policy to be effective. God did not give you insurance, but an assurance, which means the bill has been paid, no debt is owed, and no work is included or required. What is this gift that God purchased you ask? It is the gift of salvation that Paul presents here in verse eight.

4. Many blessings come with your gift, but here are some of them just to name a few. For starters, your charges are dropped in court. You are a sinner who is declared innocent in the presence of a righteous judge. You are exonerated. You are forgiven and set free. You are adopted into God's family and included in His will. You are set apart for the use of God. God's Spirit then seals you and marked you as one of His own. And, you are counted as one who is blessed by God from now until time is no more.

5. This is why you should never have snobby, braggadocios, arrogant, self-righteous churchgoers who are super religious. No matter how holy they feel they may be, their works will never be good enough to save them. Salvation comes to us by grace, through faith in Jesus. PERIOD! Nothing more and nothing less!

The Triumph That He Gives

- What is the most expensive gift you have ever received? Who bought it? Where is it now? How did you feel when you received it?

- Have you received God's gift to you? Are you certain? How do you know?

- Have you ever encountered any super holy people that sought to make you feel bad because you were not entirely like them?

- Faith in the passage means merely to believe. What are some of your fundamental beliefs you have regarding Jesus Christ, grace, faith and the Bible?

- Remember this, you are saved not because of what you do, but what you believe.

A Short Talk With God

Lord, I have received many gifts in my lifetime, but today I want to thank you for the gift of my salvation. I believe, by faith in your Son Jesus Christ and His finished work on the cross. I know that He has risen from the grave because He lives in me right now. God, I celebrate the gift that you have given me because it is much better than the wages that I have earned. Thank you Jesus for grace and I praise your name for the price you have paid just for me. In the name of Jesus, I ask this petition, Amen!

Day 3-Week 2
The Truth About Grace

Are you old enough to remember television when there were only five channels and TV signed off at midnight with pictures of fugitives that were "Wanted By The FBI" and the playing of the star spangled banner? If you can remember this, you are officially old! Nowadays television has so many channels that you cannot watch them all. In fact, you have to channel surf to see what is out there. There are stations and channels for everyone. For food lovers you have the Food Network. For sports enthusiasts, there is ESPN. For the people concerned with what is going on around the world there is CNN, HLN, and MSNBC. For old-school cartoon lovers who still appreciate Scooby-Doo, Speed Racer and Casper the Friendly Ghost, there is the Cartoon Network. For the history buff who just loves to study what happened yesterday, there is the History Channel. For those who travel and need to know what the weather is like, there is the Weather Channel.

I was channel surfing one day and came across a station that I did not know existed. It was a channel that was exclusively for people who painted. It was a little like Painting With A Twist without all of the rookie involvement and fewer canvas fatalities, if you catch my drift. Anyway, I found this one guy with an empty canvas and decided I would check him out. For two reasons, his canvas had nothing on it, so that means he could not buy a picture and then pretend that it was his work and because he just did not look like an artist to me. He appeared to be a hippy stuck in a time warp from the early 1970's.

He starts to paint by pulling up his sagging jeans, scratching his curly beard and saying, "Let's see what we've got here." It was like the Cartoon Network without all of the animation. He put several huge blobs of green paint in the middle of the canvas, followed by a blue streak right down the middle and several brown lines that appeared to be train tracks of some sort. He turned to the camera and said, "I think I need a little yellow and some pink." Pink! "What in the world is this dude doing?" I said to myself as I laughed at this fiasco he was putting together.

I grabbed a bag of Orville Redenbacher's All Natural Popcorn (my favorite snack) and continued watching and to my amazement the green blobs were now gorgeous trees. The blue streak was an amazing river. The yellow specs were now beautiful leaves on the trees as the heat of summer became the enchanting cold weather of the fall. When this guy finished, what started as a mess was a complete masterpiece! He then said something that blessed my life. He said, "What's on this canvas is a reflection of what was in my heart the whole time, you just couldn't see it, but I could."

Here is the truth about grace, your life is the canvas, and God is doing all of your painting. It may look like a mess right now but what is in His heart is going come to pass. You may not know or understand what He is doing with your life, but you do not have to because He does. Trust Him with the process.

The Treasure Of His Goodness

For we are his workmanship, created in Christ Jesus unto good works, which God hath before ordained that we should walk in them (2:10, KJV).

1. Have you ever encountered someone who you gave your best to, and for whatever reason, they just did not want you? The great news about this verse is that God is not like that. In fact, He is just the opposite. The first four words of this verse should bring comfort and consolation to you. Here is what they say, "For we are His..." The "we" in the passage describes not everybody, but every believer. If you believe in Jesus Christ, you belong to God. He wants you just like you are. He loves you, and you are His workmanship.

2. The word used for workmanship is *poimen*. This word is borrowed from Greek painters, and it was used to describe an empty canvas. Did you shout yet? Your life is God's canvas!

3. Not only are you God's workmanship, but also you were "...created in Christ Jesus unto good works..." The term created here used by Paul is the word *ktizo* in the Greek. For all practical purposes, it means to recycle or to regenerate something. It means to take what was nothing and make something out of it. By now you should be rejoicing! Here is why God specializes in taking the trash of our past and recycling it so that it becomes a portrait of grace for everyone to see in the present.

4. When did God do this you must ask? The text tells us that information, "....which God hath before ordained..." Did you hear it? God did it before you ever knew that you would exist. Well, why did God do it? So that ".... we should walk in them." Now here is the best news ever, God wants you to exist like He is your Father, Jesus is your Redeemer, and the Holy Ghost has sealed you. He wants you to walk like you are His project that is still being constructed but one day will see completion.

5. The benefit of being the workmanship of God is that there is a creator-creation concept present. You are the creation, and God is the creator. With this in mind, the creation becomes what the creator says it will be without the interference of the creation because the creator is at work!

A Short Talk With God

Lord of heaven and God of creation, treat my life like it is an empty canvas and paint my human existence in a way that everyone that I meet can see your grace on open display. In Jesus name, Amen.

Day 4-Week 2
The Truth About Grace

"Do you have a passport?" "Excuse me Sir, where is your passport?" These are hurtful, harmful words for any American to hear who may be traveling outside of the United States of America trying to get home. Okay, so here is the truth, I messed up and left my passport on the transport bus in London, and I was ready to get home. When the very kind lady in customs asked me for my passport, I reached with confidence into my bag only to realize it was not there. Have you ever been so nervous that your palms got sweaty, your knees felt weak, and your understanding became cluttered? It is what happened to me. I was looking everywhere for my passport, in my shirt pocket, my back pocket, my backpack and the purse of the woman that was standing in line behind me. No, I was not stealing! I just did not have my passport, and hers looked just like mine, so I thought she grabbed mine by mistake. Of course, she shoved me with ill will and horrible intent, but who cares? At that moment, I had an identity crisis. The legal document that proved my American citizenship was missing and I was on foreign soil.

The lady who asked me for my passport that was so helpful to me earlier had now become bitter. She had the disposition of an angry pit-bull that just had gunpowder for lunch as she grimaced and said: "Sir, please step aside.... next!" I said to myself, "Wait, I'm an American, I stand when we sing the Star Spangled Banner, and I'm ready to go home; plus you guys don't have Shipley's Do-nuts, and I'm in need of a fix here! It is a must that I get on my flight." Just then with the thought of an apple fritter on my mind, it hit me. My passport was on the transport bus. I quickly contacted the bus company, and they stopped the bus, and my passport was recovered.

I got back in line about an hour later, and that same woman looked at me and said angrily "Passport Sir!" With grace, style, class and a bit of masculine swagger I took my passport out and handed it to her, and she smiled and said, "You may enter." At that moment, I thought myself, what would you do if you got to the gates of the New Jerusalem and an angel looked at you and said, "Passport please!" What would you do? You see, there are many people who think that they are citizens of the country of heaven, but they have no passport to get them into the country.

Here is what grace says, our passport is found in the precious blood of the Lamb! You did not buy, earn, or barter your passport; the blood was applied by grace through faith to your account. The blood of the Lamb is your passport! You did not work to earn it; God graced it to you.

The Treasure Of His Goodness

Wherefore remember, that ye being in time past Gentiles in the flesh, who are called uncircumcision by that which is called the Circumcision in the flesh made by hands; that at that time ye were without Christ, being aliens from the commonwealth of Israel, and strangers from the covenants of promise, having no hope, and without God in the world: but now in Christ Jesus ye who sometimes were far off are made nigh by the blood of Christ (2:11-13, KJV).

1. An alien for many of us is a creature from outer space that does not belong here. But, here is the truth. An alien is a person that does not legally belong to a country. They are considered "strangers." As Paul writes, he makes it clear that some people thought they belonged to God because of an outward stamp of approval called "circumcision." However, Paul argues empathically, that what makes us legitimate is not what is connected to our flesh, but what is confirmed through our faith.

2. Keep this in mind, our entrance into God's Kingdom comes only through Jesus Christ, there is no other way. Jesus Christ is not a way to God; He is the way to God (John 14:1-6).

3. The blessing of knowing Jesus is that after you meet Him, you can readily remember what life was like without Him. Paul puts it on this wise, ".... and without God in the world: but now in Christ Jesus..." Words like these cause you to recall what life was like when Jesus was there for you, but you were not there for Him.

4. The greatest news of the day is this, He never changed His mind about you! Did you shout at all? Here is why you should have rejoiced; the Lord's mind is already made up about you. Your sin does not change it, your mishaps do not rearrange it, your flaws cannot turn it off, and your filthy secrets have no way of stopping it. You belong to Him no matter what your present condition looks like.

5. But how can this be? How can God love me so much? The answer is easy, you ".... are made nigh by the blood of Christ." There are numerous detergents on the market today that are used to get stains out of clothing that need to be cleaned. The problem is this; some stains just will not come out. Like horrible

stains in a precious garment, sin has stained us, and nothing seems to be able to remove its blemish. Counseling does not work, self-inflicted human torture does not get it clean, and attending worship weekly and doing good deeds does not do away with it. But the blood of the Lamb works. It washes us whiter than snow.

The Triumph That He Gives

- Take an earnest survey of your soul. Have you met Jesus Christ?

- If so, what was your life like before you came to know Him?

- What changes has knowing Jesus Christ made in your life?

- If you have not met Him or if you are not for sure, what are you waiting on? Why not get to know Him right now?

- Coming to know Him is as easy as prayerfully inviting Him into your life and admitting that He has risen from the dead and is Lord (Romans 10:9-10).

A Short Talk With God

Lord of heaven and God of glory thank you for changing my life for the better in the greatest way ever. Jesus, you have been my difference maker. Without you, my life was a disaster, but with you, every day gets sweeter as days go by. Thank you for making me a citizen of your country, and I bless you for my passport that is in full effect. In Jesus name, Amen.

Day 5-Week 2
The Truth About Grace

We had climbed into the mountains of Cafu in the country of Haiti. The climb was hot and long for someone like me who saw one flight of stairs as a daring feat. I had gone with a group of about thirty pastors from America to do mission work there. The poverty of Haiti was overwhelming. The corruption of the government, coupled with their national religion being Voodoo only helped to make things more challenging for me. As we made our way up the mountain and through the jungle, we entered into a village that was filled with Voodoo priests who saw a group of Baptist preachers as a threat. They started blowing white dust on us as we passed by.

Okay, here is a moment of honesty; I wanted to go home right then! My trip had been ruined. I came to share the Gospel, feed the hungry and help to build an orphanage for hurting children, but no one mentioned anything about Voo-Doo dust blowers wearing feathers and war paint. Can you feel me? It was chaos. It was mayhem. It was war. We were seen as the enemy, and that is how they were treating us. Just then, the bishop who was walking with us started talking to these dust blowers in their language. They went back and forth for a while. The more the bishop talked, the better things got for us. The Voodoo dust blowers started to smile at us.

Then the unthinkable happened. A huge man walked out of one of the dust blowers' tents. He was like something from a Stephen Spielberg film that you were supposed to run from. He was the chief of the village. He approached the bishop, and things seemed tense. Our bishop spoke with the chief, and it was nothing short of chaotic. After several moments of rambunctious conversation they hugged and laughed, and the chief turned around and made an announcement to his entire village, that we were now welcomed amongst his people. When our bishop returned to us, as we wiped away the dust particles that had been sprayed on us earlier that day, he told us that all was peaceful now. We were safe.

I could not help but ask the bishop how was he able to calm those people down and get the chief to accept us. He then told me that the chief was his father and because we were with his son we could not be denied the peace his father could provide.

Here is what grace says, our peace is not in a place, a provision, a payment of any sort or a portion that we feel might be owed to us. Our peace is in a person. That person is the Son, and His name is Jesus Christ.

The Treasure Of His Goodness

For he is our peace, who hath made both one, and hath broken down the middle wall of partition between us; having abolished in his flesh the enmity, even the law of commandments contained in ordinances; for to make in himself of twain one new man, so making peace; and that he might reconcile both unto God in one body by the cross, having slain the enmity thereby: and came and preached peace to you which were afar off, and to them that were nigh. For through him we both have access by one Spirit unto the Father (2:14-18, KJV).

1. Look at the first five words of the first paragraph and put them to memory. "For He is our peace…"

2. Now you have to ask yourself, "Who's He?" If you do not know who "He" is Paul is not talking to you at all. "He" can only be your peace when you know Him for yourself. Just in case you do not know who "He" is; His name is Jesus Christ, Son of the living God.

3. The word peace here is the Greek word *iraynay*, and it has nothing to do with the absence of war but the presence of a person who is greater than the problem that you currently possess.

4. Like the angry chief in the story, our problem was with God. In fact, we were the enemies of God. But God did the unthinkable. He destroyed the petition that separated divinity and humanity, and became one man with two parts. He became something time had never seen. He became the God-man. Here is how Paul said it, "…for to make in himself twain, one new man." Human enough to understand us, yet God enough to save us. Are you shouting yet? How can you hold your peace?

5. One of the benefits of having peace with God is being blessed with "…access by one Spirit unto the Father" which means you no longer need anyone to go to God for you because you can go to God for yourself. You have unlimited access into the essence of the eternal. You have access to Almighty God!

The Triumph That He Gives

- Have you ever been in real trouble? How did it make you feel?

- What if you discovered that before coming to know Jesus Christ, you were in trouble with God? How would that make you feel?

- The word "access" means you have a right to enter. In Christ, you have access to God. If God gave you access to Him, what would you do with it?

- Never forget this, the only way to destroy the barrier that separated humanity from God was for God to become human and destroy it (Phil. 2:5-11, John 1:14).

- Considering the grace of this chapter, what does it mean to have peace?

A Short Talk With God

Lord God, my soul shouts to know that I can come to you personally because of the access your Son has provided for me. Thank you for destroying the petition that once separated us and I bless your name for the peace that you have provided for me. Now God use the peace that I have in you to make me a peacemaker for those that are near me. In the powerful peace-making name of my Prince of Peace, Jesus Christ I pray, Amen!

Day 6-Week 2
The Truth About Grace

A few years ago I walked into the cathedral of Antioch to whisper a word of prayer to God. When I rose from my knees, I discovered a man standing in the foyer who appeared to be lost. He looked at me and said, "Are you the preacher here?" I looked at him carefully. I am the kind of Christian who will watch, fight and pray, so I was trying to see if this guy had something in his hands or for that matter had a pistol in his pocket. You catch my drift? After he appeared to be harmless, I answered him in the affirmative, "Yes, I'm the preacher." He then said, "I have been passing by here for a few years and I would love to see your church."

I smiled at him and said, "The church belongs to the Lord, and you can see the building, but the church is not here." He looked at me as if I were a leopard without spots and said "Huh?" I said, "The real church is not a pile of bricks, it is a precious people that God would die to save. If you're going to see the church, you'll have to come on a Sunday morning. A few more of them will be here!"

All too often people think a building is a church, but that day has come and gone. Our God no longer lives in a building built by man. God now lives in the hearts of the men that He made for Himself.

Here is what grace says, God lives in me every day. The God of all grace makes His place of holy habitation the corridors of my heart.

The Treasure Of His Goodness

Now, therefore, ye are no more strangers and foreigners, but fellow citizens with the saints, and of the household of God; and are built upon the foundation of the apostles and prophets, Jesus Christ himself being the chief corner stone; in whom all the building fitly framed together groweth unto an holy temple in the Lord: in whom ye also are builded together for an habitation of God through the Spirit (2:19-22).

1. One of the things that plague Christians today is an internal identity crisis. In short, we do not know who we are in Christ Jesus. Remember this, if you do not know who you are, you will become someone that you were never meant to be in the first place.

2. Paul gives us some wonderful snapshots of who we are in Christ. Take a moment and give each of these wonderful ideas some thought. First, Paul says we are fellow-citizens. As a believer in Jesus Christ, the bloodstained banner and the cross of Christ are our nation's flag. The Bible is our constitution, our national song is "Amazing Grace," and our leader is not a President that is elected who is serving a term. He is King of kings and Lord of lords.

3. Secondly, we are saints. The shout here is that even though saints still sin, we are no longer called sinners. We are saints! This is because God never defines you by your apparent mistakes, He calls you by your name and your approved title. You are a saint, never to be called a sinner ever again. Next, you are called the household of God. In short, you are God's house. You are the dwelling place of the Lord. In fact, you are a stone in His home, and Jesus Christ is the Chief Corner Stone that holds the entire house together.

4. Paul says that this house "...groweth unto a holy temple..." How can a house grow? It grows because the God of the house keeps adding people to it every day. This is why being saved matters so much. Your life is a precious stone in the home of the Lord (1 Peter 2:5).

5. Keep this in mind, in the Old Testament, humans built a house for God. In the New Testament, God built a house made up of humans. Are you starting to rejoice? Here is why you should. When the God of the universe needed a place to stay, He made you and said to Himself, "I'll live right here!"

The Triumph That He Gives

*   According to our study passage, how does Paul say God sees you? What words are used to describe a believer who is in Christ?

*   What does it mean for you to be a citizen of heaven?

*   As a believer in Jesus Christ, you should desire to see the church grow. In what ways do you help its growth? Do you ever share Christ with people?

*   God lives in you. How does that make you feel?

- Remember this, like you are an American with rights and privileges, you are also a citizen of glory. Live like it, love like it, forgive like it, serve like it and worship like it.

A Short Talk With God

Lord of glory, make my heart your dwelling place. Consume me with your love, favor me with your grace, keep me with your power and sustain me with your kindness. I belong to you and you alone. In the name of Jesus, Amen!

Chapter 3

Hey Preacher, I've Got Something To Say, I've Got A Story To Tell!

Week 3

The Grace Of His Ability

Day 1-Week 3
The Truth About Grace

There are times I wish that I could have my own reality TV show. Sometimes things happen to me that are just amazing. There is never a dull moment. In fact, when I find myself feeling a tad bit melancholy, I lift my spirit by going to HEB on the corner of College Street and 11th Street in Beaumont, Texas. Wait, I know what you are thinking. I am going to the store to buy snacks that I don't need when I should be fasting, and you're right. But, that is not the only reason why I go. You see, when I get to HEB people have a habit of stopping me to share their testimonies. It happens every time. Some of my closest friends no longer grocery shop with me because they want to get in and get out, but when I go I want to hear the stories.

I will never forget it as long as I live. Hurricane Harvey made landfall in Texas on Friday, August 25, 2017. The rain started and did not stop until we felt like Noah without an Ark in Southeast Texas. HEB opened its doors for limited operations to allow people to grab a few items and I made my way there. I did not need anything, but I knew that it would happen. I saw everyone that I knew in Beaumont or at least it felt like it. While hugging a family who had evacuated to Beaumont from Houston, I heard a voice right behind me that sounded like a head football coach on the sideline who needed to get a lineman's attention who was just guilty of a holding penalty.

Here is what the voice shouted to me, "Hey preacher, I've got something to say, I've got a story to tell!" I turned slowly around, and there sat a rather portly gentleman in a motorized wheelchair looking right at me. He said, "Yeah Reverend Adolph, I said, I've got something to say!" I reached to shake his hand, and he stood up out of his shiny motorized wheelchair. He said, "I don't need no wheelchair, I use this thang cause I like the way it rides. It's smooth. Do you recognize me?" I said, "No sir, but you have my undivided attention." He said, "That's because the last you time you saw me I was in ICU at St. Elizabeth Hospital with a tube in my throat. He said, "Rev. you prayed for me. I don't know how you got to my room, but you prayed for me. God healed my body; I did not say you healed me. I said you prayed. And here I am." I looked and said "Woooooooooooowwwwww!" He said, "I ain't scared of Harvey. Tell him I said come on! I have been through much worse and if God could see me through what I have been through, I know that I'm going to make it."

Here is the truth about grace; every real Christian has a story to tell. Your story may not be mine, and mine admittedly may not be yours, but we both have one that says, "God is an able God!"

The Treasure Of His Goodness

For this cause I Paul, the prisoner of Jesus Christ for you Gentiles, if ye have heard of the dispensation of the grace of God which is given me to you-ward: how that by revelation he made known unto me the mystery; (as I wrote afore in few words, whereby, when ye read, ye may understand my knowledge in the mystery of Christ), (Eph. 3:1-4, KJV).

1. Paul is about to start telling us a little of his story. He defines himself as "the prisoner of Jesus Christ for you Gentiles." By this he means, that he was doing what he wanted to do and God grabbed him while he was on the Damascus Road and turned his life upside down, so that he could flip it, right side up (Read Acts 9:1-9).

2. The Greek word for prisoner used in this passage is **desmios**, and it is used to describe a man who has been placed under arrest. If you have never been arrested, you cannot relate, but if you have, you can. Arrests are rarely simple. They are disruptive and overwhelming. They are radical at best. Here's what we can

conclude about Paul's conversion and God's power; there are times when God just radically changes a person and your life after an encounter with Him is never the same again.

3. Remember this phrase, "...the dispensation of the grace of God..." This sentence is the best news a Christian will ever hear. Here is why. A dispensation is a period in which God dealt with humanity in a certain way. In short, a dispensation is an arrangement of time defined by God that details how He will treat us. The era of time that we live in is the period called grace!

4. Grace comes from the Greek word *charis.* It means to favor heavily, to grant, bestow, give and allow. Therefore, everything that we have has been graced to us by the goodness of God. We have earned nothing at all.

5. Grace to the people of the Old Testament was a mystery, but to the Church of the New Testament, grace is a way life. We are saved by grace, blessed through grace, held by grace, sustained by grace, kept by grace and showered by grace.

The Triumph That He Gives

*   What is your story? What has God done for you?

*   What was your conversion experience like? Was it like that of the Apostle Paul's where God put you under arrest?

*   Why do you think God gives us so much grace (James 4: 7)?

*   In what ways have you experienced the grace of God? Be specific.

*   Remember, the grace of God demands a response. Grace in Latin is gratia. We borrow our English word gratitude from it. Therefore, wherever there is grace received there should be gratitude produced.

A Short Talk With God

Lord, if you gave me what I deserved I would not have anything, but because of your grace, you have caused me to prosper in spite of all that I fall short of. Thank you Jesus for grace. I am forever indebted to you for the grace you have bestowed upon my life. My solemn petition to you this day in prayer is for you to give me a chance to brag on your grace every time I get a chance. In Jesus Christ, Amen!

FROM THE DIRECTORS CHAIR

Click or type this link into your browser to view: https://youtu.be/vTLnC1IFEyA

1. Dionese admits that she needs a "dose of Jesus." Have you ever been there before? In a place where you needed more of God and less of you?

2. What role do you think God's grace has to do with you being refueled and refilled?

3. One of the things that make grace so amazing is God's ability to save us from sin and forgive us from human error and personal flaw. Have you ever had a particular weakness that was ungodly? What role did God's grace play for you?

4. There are times that our plans and God's plans for us are radically different. Why do you think this happens so often?

5. Never forget this, God's grace is not a ticket to sin; it is a right to live holy. With this in mind, there are times that we just waste grace. In what ways has this happened to you? Have you overcome it? If so, how did God help you do it?

Day 2-Week 3
The Truth About Grace

A young thug was murdered in Beaumont. He had been shot six times at point-blank range. His relatives were members of Antioch so I allowed the family to hold his funeral at the church so that we could give support to their grieving family. When I arrived at church for this young man's funeral service, I passed by a car in our parking lot where the smell of marijuana was coming from those who were puffing and passing on the inside. Okay, I was offended and started to call the police, but I didn't. I got to the back door where I enter the building most of the time, and there stood a young man who was ushering. However, he was not apart of my Ushers Ministry. He was wearing sagging blue shorts, a baseball cap, and a Dallas Cowboys football jersey with the tags on it and a mouth filled with gold teeth. By now I'm like, "What the heck is going on here!"?

I looked up, and there were women in spandex dress everywhere. I thought I was in the club. All I was missing was the smell of cigarette smoke and the clinking sound of liquor bottles tapped by the bartender. Okay, I tried to act like I didn't see it right? I walk into the cathedral of the church, and there sat six pallbearers wearing baseball caps, sunglasses, sporting a marijuana joint behind their right ear! I look in the coffin, and the deceased young man has a twenty-dollar bag of weed in his hand (And don't ask me how I, the great holy Pastor would know that) and a cigarette lighter to boot.

I turned around in anger to put them all out of "my church, " and that is when the still small voice of God spoke to me and said, "This is my house, and I invited them. I decided to bring them to you since you have been too busy to go and get them for me."

Okay, let's just clear the air. There are times we do not want to be affiliated with people that are not like us. For whatever reason, we see ourselves as just a little bit better than everyone else.

Here is the truth about grace; if God's grace was sufficient for you, it is good enough for everyone.

The Treasure Of His Goodness

Which in other ages was not made known unto the sons of men, as it is now revealed unto his holy apostles and prophets by the Spirit; that the Gentiles should be fellow heirs, and of the same body, and partakers of his promise in Christ by the gospel: whereof I was made a minister, according to the gift of the grace of God given unto me by the effectual working of his power.

Unto me, who am less than the least of all saints, is this grace given, that I should preach among the Gentiles the unsearchable riches of Christ (3:5-8, KJV).

1. In every socio-cultural environment ever known to humankind, there have been found people who thought they were better than other people. When this happens you always have matters of discrimination: haves vs. the have-nots, GED's vs. Ph.D.'s, and the list goes on. But, keep this in mind; God's grace is for everyone.

2. Paul had a season of his life where, as a Pharisee and a Jew, he just knew that he was better than the Gentiles. But, God said, "Not so!"

3. The "...gift of the grace of God..." given to you is not so that you can take it and boast to others about how holy, flawless, righteous and wonderful you are. It is given to you so that you can tell others that need it where to find it. Paul declares that grace was given to him so that he could ".... preach among the Gentiles, the unsearchable riches of Christ." You cannot tell me how good the catfish is unless you have tasted it. You cannot tell me how great the gumbo is unless you have had at least one bowl. Likewise, you cannot share the grace that you have received until you celebrate the grace that you have been given.

4. The tension of Paul's day was between Gentiles nations (those who were uncircumcised and non-Jews) and the Jews (those that were chosen by God, who bore the mark of circumcision in the flesh and who practiced keeping the law but broke it in some way every day).

5. Please know this, the law of God is good. However, it was only given to humankind to prove one point. Here is the point; we all need God's grace!

The Triumph That He Gives

- Be honest, have you ever looked down your nose at someone because you thought you were just a little bit better than they were?

- As a Christian, there are some sins that you have been delivered from, and whether you know it or not, there are some sins that you still commit. What role do you think that grace plays in both instances?

- If the grace that God has given you could be put on display what would your grace look like?

- Why do you think most people are incredibly judgmental?

- Church folks can be the most conscientious people in the world. Keep this in mind, Jesus died for sin, but sinners did not crucify Him, religious people did. With this in mind, why do you think churchgoers are so quick to need grace and extremely slow to give it to others?

A Short Talk With God

O Lord, as I pray this petition my life is in need of more of your grace. I can see where I'm doing well, but in my attempt to do well I know that I am not good enough. I never get it all right. Lord take my shortcomings and my human errors and cover them with your grace. And, Lord give me an opportunity to tell someone where your grace is located who needs it like I do. In Jesus name, Amen.

Day 3-Week 3
The Truth About Grace

I grew up watching the Price Is Right! I loved it. Bob Barker was smooth, and those ladies on stage with him were always the cutest ever. I liked hearing the announcer call the next contestant. When those people listened to their names called they would scream, jump, shout and run down that aisle and they would not have won one thing yet. Just the sheer excitement of having their names called brought them to the point of nearly losing their minds.

On one occasion, I made my way to the Price Is Right studio so I could be a contestant myself. Don't judge me, but I couldn't help it. I just felt like God wanted me to be a grand prizewinner and take home the big showcase. It was retribution and compensation for watching the show for nearly two decades right? Plus, I promised Him that if I won, I would bring Him the tithe (Pray for me please). Okay, so here's the truth, I did not win, my name was not called, and it took nearly eight hours to get into the studio just to be involved in the live recording.

While sitting in the studio, I fell in love with the game where the contestant has to choose a curtain without knowing what's behind it. Bob Barker said, "Will it be curtain number one, number two or number three?" I loved it because what's behind the curtain remains a mystery but when the curtain is lifted the mystery becomes history because the secret is then revealed.

So it is with grace! For many years, through the days of the Prophets and Seers, grace was a mystery. But, when Jesus Christ died on the cross and rose again three days later, the curtain was lifted, and the age of grace became the place for our sins to be covered!

Here is the truth about grace; it is no longer a secret. The mystery of grace has been revealed because the depravity of humanity demands the gracious kindness of God's divinity.

The Treasure Of His Goodness

And to make all men see what is the fellowship of the mystery, which from the beginning of the world hath been hidden in God, who created all things by Jesus Christ: to the intent that now unto the principalities and powers in heavenly places might be known by the church the manifold wisdom of God, according to the eternal purpose which he purposed in Christ Jesus our Lord: in whom we have boldness and access with confidence by the faith of him. Wherefore I desire that ye faint not at my tribulations for you, which is your glory (3:9-13, KJV).

1. The Greek word Paul uses for the term mystery is ***musterion***. Greek actors used it on stage that knew what their scripts held, while those that watched had to wait until the end to see what would happen.

2. When Paul calls something a mystery, he is not saying; I don't know how it works. What he is saying is this, I know how it works because I was once in the dark but now I have been brought into the light.

3. As a believer in Jesus Christ, you have the script in your hand. Our script is given to us in the Bible. We do not have to wonder how things are going to play out. We know already.

4. Keep this in mind; to be forewarned is to be forearmed. Now that you know, you should live as you know. This is why Paul tells the Ephesian Church to have "…. boldness and access with confidence…" People who know up front should always win in the end.

5. The most significant news of the day is this, grace has been given and made known to us because God desires to have fellowship with us. Jews could not understand how God, who is so transcendent, (YWHW) could have fellowship with sinners like us. It was a mystery. But that mystery concluded when Christ commenced on earth with His birth.

The Triumph That He Gives

*   If anyone ever tells you, they have God all figured out you should run. God is a perpetual mystery. With this in mind, if you could ask God just one question what would you ask Him and why?

*   The fellowship of saints is something that the Bible teaches that we should do. In what ways has being near other believers in Jesus Christ helped you?

*   God has revealed Himself to us in the person of Jesus Christ. What have you learned about Jesus that makes you certain about who He is? What is an area of spiritual certainty regarding the Lord for you?

- There are times when even the greatest of believers struggle with God. This is because there are times God allows things to happen that we do not understand. Has God ever allowed something to happen in your life that you did not understand? What was it?

- Remember this, you may not know all there is to know about God, but it's not what you don't know about God that keeps you when life has questions, it is what you do know. You win with resting upon the truths that the open curtain of the Bible grants you.

A Short Talk With God

God, you are awesome. I love the fact that you have revealed to me the age of grace and I genuinely thank you for the grace you have provided. I also know that you are a mystery. God help me to trust you with the parts of my life that I do not understand and strengthen me in areas of my faith that I do understand. Grow me in your grace and bless me with the privilege of holding your hand until life ends or the rapture happens. In Jesus name, Amen!

Day 4-Week 3
The Truth About Grace

To have the prayers of a loving father is wonderful; to have the prayers of a caring mother is life changing; to have the prayers of a faithful friend can be a source of encouragement; to have the prayers of the saints can be a blessing, but to have the prayers of your Pastor can lead to healing and deliverance. In short, there are times when you should want and need the intercessory prayer of your Pastor to God on your behalf and say, "Lord, your servant needs you, and I'm here on their behalf."

I once had a parishioner whose name was Lisa. She had suffered four miscarriages while trying to have a child. Her doctor had recommended adoption to her, but this woman had great faith in the Lord Jesus Christ. She came to me privately and said, "Pastor I can pray for myself, but I need your prayers on this. I'm pregnant, and the doctors want me to terminate the pregnancy because of my previous miscarriages, but I'm believing God that my son will be born healthy. His name is Isaiah, and he will be God's light for his generation." I prayed for her. We prayed together. She wept at the altar, and I prayed until I could not pray anymore." Six months later, Isaiah was born strong and healthy to the glory of God!

Here is the truth about grace, God does not have to answer our sacred supplications, but He does. Grace says, "Prayer does work!"

The Treasure Of His Goodness

For this, cause I bow my knees unto the Father of our Lord Jesus Christ, of whom the whole family in heaven and earth is named (3:14-15, KJV).

1. Notice that verse one of chapter three and verse fourteen of chapter three both begin with the same four words, "For this cause I..." Paul was so busy telling us his testimony that he lost track of his thoughts. Have you ever been so excited to tell someone what the Lord has done for you that you forgot what you were saying and had to get back on track? This is what happens here.

2. However, the great Apostle now knows what he wants to say and he says to the church I am praying for you. In fact, he is specific. He says I'm praying "...unto the Father of our Lord Jesus Christ..." This is so rich. Paul is not burning a candle or lighting incense; he is talking to God the Father in the name and authority of God the Son. It is worthy of mentioning that any time you pray to

the Father in the name of the Son, that prayer carries the authority of the Son when it comes to the Father.

3. The blessing of this prayer is that it comes from a Pastor's heart to God for His people who are described in the text as the "...the whole family in heaven..." Why does Paul call us a family? We all have the same Father. We all have the same older brother in Jesus Christ, and we all have flaws and need the grace on our side.

4. The opening phrase of this text, "For this cause I..." is written in the Greek tense that suggests the action starts and does not stop. In other words, Paul's bowing for the people of God is perpetual. He is always praying for them. It is something that he does over and over and over again.

5. The reason for this is serious but very simple. Every real Pastor wants the people that are under their leadership blessed by God in every way. So, real Pastors spend time acting as intercessors and praying for those that follow them as they follow Christ.

The Triumph That He Gives

- If you are a Christian, do you have a Pastor? If you do not have a Pastor, you need one.

- Have you ever gone through a time so severe that you needed a Pastor to pray for you? If so, what happened?

- What role does your Pastor play in your spiritual life?

- If you could ask your Pastor to pray for you, what you would like for your Pastor to pray for?

- Remember this, a Pastor is not a magician but should be a servant. To ask your Pastor for prayer is a blessing for you and a benefit for him.

A Short Talk With God

Lord, I am thankful for my Pastor. I know that my Pastor prays for me, but right now I lift my Pastor to you and I ask you to lead, feed, direct, protect, instruct and inspire my Pastor. Continue to speak to my Pastor's heart so that my Pastor can speak to me on your behalf. Most importantly, keep your hands on my Pastor. Erase and delete personal sins, renew and refresh spiritual vitality and lead my Pastor so that He can undoubtedly lead the church of which I am a part. In Jesus name, Amen!

Day 5-Week 3
The Truth About Grace

There are so many people that approach me and ask for my prayers. It is my joy to do it. On one occasion, a young man asked me to pray for him. I paused and asked him what did he need from God? He paused and thought for a moment. He then said, "I need so much right now I don't have time to give you my list. Just tell the Lord that I'm ready for Him to use me but I don't know what to do next." What a prayer request! I walked away from him rushing to my car but felt an urgent need to go back and pray for him right then. We prayed in the parking lot of Exygon, a workout facility in Beaumont. The presence of God consumed us, and we both knew it. I feel confident in saying that whatever he needed from God that day, he received.

Here is the truth about grace, there comes a time when you say, God, I'm ready for you to use me and I just don't know what to do next. The blessing of such a prayer request is this; the grace of the Lord has kept you and protected you for such a time as this.

The Treasure Of His Goodness

That he would grant you, according to the riches of his glory, to be strengthened with might by his Spirit in the inner man; that Christ may dwell in your hearts by faith; that ye, being rooted and grounded in love, may be able to comprehend with all saints what is the breadth, and length, and depth, and height; and to know the love of Christ, which passeth knowledge, that ye might be filled with all the fullness of God (3:16-19, KJV).

1. This is one of the most moving prayers in the entire Bible. It is a prayer to God for the people that are within the confines of the church.

2. Let's examine it and rejoice together. Paul asks the Lord to strengthen them spiritually. He calls it the "inner man." **Krateioo** is the word choice here, and it means strength that comes from another source. For example, a light bulb is good, but it uses the strength of the electric company to light up a room. Paul says Lord give them some of what you are.

3. Paul then asks the Lord to allow "...Christ to dwell in your hearts by faith..." The word dwell here means to live in a house. The shout here is that there is a

difference between a house and tent. A tent is temporary, but a home is meant to be permanent. Paul says to set up residence in their lives and never move.

4. He then asks the Lord cause them to be "…. rooted and grounded in love…" this is so moving. Why? Because the most painful thing for a Pastor to endure is when his people do not love each other. It hurts deeply. Paul says cause them to love each other, which is the greatest commandment of them all.

5. Lastly, Paul prays that the people he leads may, "…. comprehend what the breadth, and length, and depth, and height; and to know the love of Christ…. that they might be filled with all the fullness of God." Notice the dimensions given here in this text. Breadth, depth, height, and length. When you consider each of these you conclude that its geometric construct is the cross! Paul says keep them near the cross so that they might be filled (*playroo*) with who God is. Please notice what Paul does not pray for. He does not pray for each member to drive a Cadillac or for each person to be rich. He prays for them to be so near the cross that they live filled with the presence of God.

The Triumph That He Gives

- Take a moment and survey your soul. How strong in the faith are you?

- How would you rejoice if you discovered that your strength is always insufficient, but God is going to give you some of His strength just to make it?

- Have you ever been around Christians that did not love each other for whatever reason? What was the problem? Did you pray for them? Why or why not?

- When you see a cross what comes to mind?

- Remember this; God wants you to be so filled with His presence that you reveal His person to the people that come near you.

A Short Talk With God

Eternal God my Father, I thank you right now for the cross of your only begotten Son, Jesus Christ. When He died at Cavalry for me, it was a love that I had never encountered. Thank you for loving me. I need your love, and I need your strength. Keep me so near you that I hear your voice, feel your presence and obey your every command each moment, each day of my life. In the name of Jesus, Amen!

Day 6-Week 3
The Truth About Grace

I was blessed by God to grow up with parents who believed firmly in Jesus Christ. New Hope Missionary Baptist Church in Houston, Texas is where I accepted Christ and was baptized. As a young kid growing up in the church, I noticed there were always certain phrases that my father used while preaching that moved the entire congregation. I mean things would go from boring to shouting if he said them. And when he repeated them enough times something similar to Pentecost was going to break loose.

One Sunday morning the air conditioner was broken, and it was hot outside. People were fanning and ready to go home. It was one of those worship services when people wanted a short sermon, a quick offering and a fast song so that they could get to the benediction and get out of there. My father stood up and said, "I do not have a sermon today." We all knew what that meant. He was about to ramble for the next hour or so on every subject known to humankind. My dad then said to us, as we sat losing weight due to the sauna we were sitting in, "God only gave me one phrase for you today, and I'm going to give it to you, and we can go home." He closed his Bible and said "The Lord laid this on my heart early this morning when I arose. I got up and tried to shake it but I couldn't so I'll just tell you what He said. He's Able!" As soon as he said it the church just lost it. Hands started waving, hats began falling, and people started shouting.

When we got in the car after church my dad turned on the air, and it felt like Jack Frost was nipping at my nose, but I wanted him to bite me. When my sweat finally dried up, I ask my Dad what happened today at church. Why so much shouting and crying and clapping? My father said, "Bobby (my nickname), I only deliver the mail. I tell the people what God tells me to tell them. Today He wanted them to know that He was able!" He said, "The shouting you heard was not them hearing me, they heard from God, and that was their response to Him!"

Here is the truth about grace, God is still able! PERIOD!

The Treasure Of His Goodness

Now unto him, that is able to do exceeding abundantly above all that we ask or think,

1. This is a verse that you should commit to memory. It is powerful, practical and poignant. It declares clearly, the ability and authority of God.

2. The passage shows us a pyramid of God's potency. Paul says that God "is" and believe this or not, that's enough. To say that God "is" is to say that He is our everything. But Paul then goes deeper. He says that He is "...is able to do, exceeding abundantly above all that we ask or think..." Each word of this passage builds on the next to the point that you discover there is nothing that God cannot do.

3. However, notice where His power is seen and encountered. It ".... worketh in us..." The blessing here is this; His power works in us to cause us to become the creation He wants us to be.

4. And why is God doing this? Because He desires His glory to be made manifest in the church. In short, when you look at the church you find grace at work, and when you see grace at work, you cannot help but give God the glory that He deserves.

5. The blessing of this verse is that the glory of our God will last forever! And, ever! And, ever!

The Triumph That He Gives

- Take a moment and think about God. How big He is, how awesome He is, how powerful He is and then ask yourself this question. Is there anything too hard for God?

- When you hear the words "...able to do exceeding abundantly above all that we ask or think..." what comes to your mind?

- Have you ever experienced God's power working in your life? If so, what did He do?

- What do you think God's power and God's grace have in common?

- Remember this, God's grace is a manifestation of God's power that is undeniable. It is why all of the glory belongs to Him! He alone is worthy!

A Short Talk With God

Lord Jesus, you are my everything. Life for me makes no sense without you. But, with you, every day gets sweeter as days go by. My desire each day is to live a life that you can receive glory from because I know that the glory belongs to you. You have blessed me with everything that I have. I love you with my whole heart. In Jesus name, Amen!

Chapter 4

Don't Get It Twisted, I'm Meek Not Weak!

Week 4
The Grace Of Effective Ministry

Day 1-Week 4
The Truth About Grace

Have you ever had someone mistreat you? Did it get on your last nerve? Did it make you want to reach out and grab them in the name of the Lord? Let's be open and honest for a moment. Some people can get on your last nerve. There are still other folks who can take your kindness for granted and your meekness for weakness. It was the fall of 1989, and my sabbatical away from church was coming to a close. Okay so let me be transparent for a moment, I left the church for a good while. I saw no need to go. After all, the people there were great at sinning. So I figured if you are going to sin why even bother going to church. It was so amazing, the sins of church folks drove me away from the church, and my own sin brought me back. Whatever the case, I was back in church full time, and I had been helping a friend of mine get back on his feet. This was the kind of friend I would give my last twenty dollars and split a Whopper with cheese with.

All of a sudden that joker just started talking crazy to me. To make matters worse, this rascal caused me even more hassle when he started lying to me and talking about me behind my back. Has this ever happened to you before? It is a real test of your love for Jesus Christ, like for real. So, I had taken all that I wanted to take. I planned a tremendous retaliatory measure for him. It was going to be a ghetto-fabulous-coke bottle attack with the lights on right across the forehead, coupled with a total flurry of jabs to the face, a metal pipe across the lower leg directly above the shin and just below the knee. Add to that a reoccurring punch to the upper torso just in case he thought about getting up from the floor. In short, I had planned an old fashion beat down for him that was going to be such a blessing and a stress reliever for me. After all, I saw this joker as the source of my pain.

I picked up my devotional lesson on a Tuesday morning, and it read "Don't Get It Twisted, I'm Meek Not Weak." I closed the book and walked off. But, the Lord compelled me to sit and read it. I was so outdone. The lesson was about how real Christians are meek because they have submitted their lives to Jesus and how meekness is power under control. I closed the journal, asked the Lord to help me and ran right into my so-called friend. I wanted to get him, but I did not do it. I had the power, ability, wherewithal, skill, experience, and technique to do a great job at getting him good, but I did not do it.

Here is the truth about grace; to follow Jesus is not about how much you go to church. It is about a lifestyle that says I live in total submission to Him, so I am meek, and not weak!

The Treasure Of His Goodness

I therefore, the prisoner of the Lord, beseech you that ye walk worthy of the vocation wherewith ye are called, with all lowliness and meekness, with longsuffering, forbearing one another in love; endeavoring to keep the unity of the Spirit in the bond of peace (4:1-3, KJV).

1. Check this out; Paul does not call himself an Apostle here; he refers to himself again as a "prisoner." It is the Greek term *desmios,* and it means to live on lockdown. This is so rich! It suggests that if you are going to be a follower of Jesus Christ, you must put the old you in prison under His authority, while Christ lives His life through you.

2. Notice if you will, that Paul urges every believer (beseech) to "…. walk worthy of the vocation wherewith ye are called…" However, you cannot walk worthy if you do not submit daily. In short, you will never serve what you are not surrendered to.

3. Now here is what is so deep. The root of surrender produces fruit in the faith. The fruit is described in this pericope. Here is what a surrendered life in Jesus Christ provides: lowliness means to be humble on purpose. Meekness is the Greek term *praotetos* and it is the picture of a horse with a bit in its mouth. The horse

is strong enough to kill its rider, but the bit in his mouth keeps him under control. Long-suffering does not mean to suffer a long time. It means to have spiritual restraint.

4. Forbearing one another in love suggest that you work as the person who keeps someone from falling flat on their back. You become one who props people up, and you do it not because they will owe a favor in return. You do it just because you love God. In short, you become not only a peacekeeper, but also a peacemaker.

5. Keep this in mind; it is impossible to possess any of the fruit of this passage without being wholly rooted in the grace of total surrender.

The Triumph That He Gives

*   It is possible to be a follower of Jesus Christ and not be surrendered to Him. Take a moment and examine your own heart. Now ask yourself this question: Am I surrendered to Jesus Christ?

*   If not, why? What is stopping you from being His "prisoner"?

*   Do you consider yourself to be meek? One quick way to tell is to examine the fruit that comes from your life. If you have strange fruit growing in your life like jealousy, envy, hypocrisy, and unforgiveness meekness may be far from you.

*   Are you the messy type? Be honest. If you are, you should strongly consider changing that today and here is why. There is only one way to kill a kingdom, and it is to divide it. Mess-makers have a special gift. People listen to them. So why use a gift negatively and divide people, when the same gift could be used positively to unite people? It just makes sense to use a gift like that to bring people together.

*   Remember this, none of this is possible unless you surrender to Jesus Christ.

A Short Talk With God

Lord of heaven, I bow and pray to you right now, and I ask you to use my life for your glory. I know that there are areas of my life that are not under your authority yet. At this moment, I submit them to you. In fact, Lord I lay my life on the altar of sacrifice so that you can use me in any way you see fit. I will be your prisoner, just please be my Master, Savior, Christ, and Lord. In Jesus name, Amen!

FROM THE DIRECTORS CHAIR

Click or type this link into your browser to view: https://youtu.be/DTYBeDhalOc

1. It is pretty clear that Dionese is struggling with the issue of total surrender. What do you think she is doing wrong?

2. Every believer has a past. What past does it seem that Dionese and the pastor share in common?

3. There are times when people will do most anything to get what they want. This includes causing chaos and killing peace. Have you ever seen this happen before in your life?

4. Family mess hurts, and church mess can wreak havoc. Have you ever been affiliated or associated with discord in either your own family or church family? What happened? What role did you play in trying to mend matters?

5. In every institution on the face of the earth, there is a mess, and there is the movement of forward progress. The best results in the Kingdom of God for Christians is to minimize mess and maximize ministry. With this in mind, what could you do to make your ministry life at church better?

Day 2-Week 4

The Truth About Grace

The story was told of a little girl who would often look at a church building with a steeple on it and then ask her mother, "Mommy what's that?" To which her mother would reply, "Honey, that is God's house." On one occasion the little girl noticed several churches located right next door to each other. There was a Methodist church, a Pentecostal Church and a Baptist Church sitting side by side. The child then said, "Mommy if all of these are God's houses which one does He live in?"

It can be slightly confusing when you think about it. Catholics are saying the rosary, while Baptists are singing hymns and quoting the scriptures. Methodists are doing their thing with the liturgy. The Church of Christ is singing a cappella and claiming that they are the only ones going to heaven and Pentecostals are dancing and speaking in unknown tongues. That little girl asked an excellent question, "Mommy.... which house does God live in?" Ready for the answer? Here it is. There is only one church! The one that is blood washed, water baptized, Holy Ghost filled, Bible-believing, faithfully serving, sharing the Gospel and waiting on the rapture. The denomination is just like a microwave oven; it is man-made. But, the church of the living God belongs solely to Lord Himself. There is only one church; only one bride; only one people; who through the cross belong to Him.

Here is the truth about grace; there is only one way to be saved, and that is to be born-again (John 3:1-16). It is this oneness that every believer, regardless of the denomination has in common.

The Treasure Of His Goodness

There is one body, and one Spirit, even as ye are called in one hope of your calling; one Lord, one faith, one baptism, one God and Father of all, who is above all, and through all, and in you all (4:4-6, KJV).

1. This passage is exciting. It kills division and promotes unity like no other passage in the Bible. In fact, there is a reoccurring motif that flows through this passage like a royal purple cord would through a beautiful white quilt. It is the word "one."

2. Look carefully at this passage. The word "one" is mentioned seven times.

3. Each time the word "one" is used it presents the notion of being exclusive. It could read "one and only". It also connotes and suggests that the "one" used is also inclusive in that it belongs to God.

4. The blessing of the oneness of the faith is that it unites Christians on the issues that matter most.

5. For many years this passage was used to formulate what was known as the Apostles' Creed. This creed carries with it the core, crux, and center of the Christian faith. It is as follows,

> *I believe in God, the Father almighty,*
> *creator of heaven and earth.*
> *I believe in Jesus Christ, God's only Son, our Lord,*
> *who was conceived by the Holy Spirit,*
> *born of the Virgin Mary,*
> *suffered under Pontius Pilate,*
> *was crucified, died, and was buried;*
> *He descended into hell.*
> *On the third day he rose again;*
> *He ascended into heaven,*
> *He is seated at the right hand of the Father,*
> *and he will come to judge the living and the dead.*
> *I believe in the Holy Spirit,*
> *the holy Catholic Church,*
> *the communion of saints,*
> *the forgiveness of sins,*
> *the resurrection of the body,*
> *and the life everlasting. Amen.*

The Triumph That He Gives

- Often the oneness of the local church is threatened by many forms of division. What kind of division threatens your local church?

- There is a difference between unity and uniformity. What do you think the difference is?

- Paul is fond of the phrase "hope of your calling." When he says this, it means that our total anticipation regarding what God has promised us as Christians lies completely in the person of Jesus Christ. How does this understanding impact you personally?

- What are your feelings about denominations? Be open and honest.

- Remember this; God is a lover of variety. This is why we have the colors of a rainbow. It is also why there are so many different kinds of fish in the sea. For our God, variety is the spice of life. How does denominationalism make variety a good thing? How does denominationalism divide the church?

A Short Talk With God

O God, Father of all creation, make your church on earth one, as you are one in heaven. In the name of Jesus, Amen!

Day 3-Week 4
The Truth About Grace

I want to share a pet peeve with you, but I do not want you to judge me, okay! Wait, if you are the judgmental type skip this section and just go to the section below labeled "The Treasure of His Goodness" because what I am about to share is not that nice, but I need to say it. So here it goes. I hate when I'm invited to gatherings and they fix your plate like it was made for troops in Desert Storm living on rations. There, I said it. For the slim physically fit people reading this devotional you may feel that I overeat. To assume such may be correct. However, here is my point, why invite a two hundred and seventy-eight-pound man to eat and then act like there is a severe shortage of turkey legs in the kitchen. Catch my drift?

I have been places where I have heard people arguing as they dished up plates about how much food to put on each plate and that's too much. It is so nerve-racking to me. It ruins my appetite, and that takes quite a bit of damage to do. On the contrary, nothing makes me happier than a cook standing in the kitchen door with her hand on her hip, sweat on her brow and a towel dangling over her shoulder looking at me as if to say, "So you think you can eat, huh!" I shout spiritually when I see a table that is spread, and you feel like a mosquito at a backyard party full of people wearing shorts: you know what to do, but you just don't know where to bite first.

I went to a family reunion in Beaumont not long ago where I became an instant cousin. It happened at the moment they started bringing food out of the kitchen and sitting it out for people to dig in. The matriarch made an announcement that made my soul rejoice. She merely said, "Y'all come eat and don't be bashful, there's more where that came from!"

Here is the truth about grace, it never runs out. In fact, God's grace did not start with you, and it will not stop with you. The Lord's grace covers a multitude of sins. This includes yours, mine and everyone else that you can think of.

The Treasure Of His Goodness

But unto every one of us is given grace according to the measure of the gift of Christ (4:7, KJV).

1. This verse is only for "us." It is what you would call an exclusive inclusivism. It is only for those of us who believe in Jesus Christ.

2. One of the benefits of belief according to this passage is that you are "…given grace…" It is **didomi charis** in the Greek, which means that God did it without you requesting that He do it. The good news about this grace is that it is the grace that is applied to human sin and personal error. Are you shouting yet? Take a moment and look carefully at your sins and personal faults, human failures, and wrongdoings. Now imagine this in your heart, God covered your sins with His grace!

3. A good question to ask here is "how much grace will you need to cover all of your sins?" Here is the answer, "…. the measure of the Gift of Christ." In other words, God will give you what you need at the time that you need it.

4. Keep this in mind; the words that begin with the letter "g" in this passage are all a benefit and blessing to you. The "g" words in the text are given, grace and gift. All of these terms come from God who loves you without restraint. It is His proof that He loves you.

5. Never forget this, grace is never a right to live wrong, but it is the reason you should want to live right.

The Triumph That He Gives

- If each of your sins cost one dollar before you could be out of debt with God, how many dollars would you need to be debt free? How much would your sins cost?

- You have more unknown sins than you have known sins. So multiply the number of your known sins in question one times five. Now how much would you need?

- How would you rejoice if you learned right now that when Jesus Christ died on the cross, He applied "the measure" of grace to your life so that your past, present, and future debts are all paid in full? How does that make you feel?

- Keep this in mind; you will never beat God giving, no matter how hard you try. Usually, when we hear phrases like this, we think about money. But, from here on, you should consider mercy and grace. Why? The grace of the Lord Jesus Christ is like the pots from the kitchen at the family reunion that I attended. "There is always more where that came from!"

- Do you ever feel like you owe God something that you can never repay? Why do you think this way? What do you think God wants from you in return?

A Short Talk With God

Eternal Master, when I consider my life and all that is in it I have concluded that I am inadequate. However, when I think about your grace and how much of it you have given to me, I know that you are more than enough. You are completely sufficient. Lord my prayer right now is for you to take my human inadequacy and meet it with the grace of your divine sufficiency and make me your own. Be merciful with your hand, loving with your touch, patient with my progress, slow with your wrath, long-suffering with your anger and discipline, and gracious with your provisions that never cease. In the name of Jesus, I pray, Amen.

Day 4-Week 4
The Truth About Grace

Floyd "Big Money" Mayweather has made boxing history. It does not matter whether critics like him or he is booed by haters; his place in boxing history is etched in stone. His professional record is now a whopping fifty wins and zero losses. In short, it can be said that Mayweather is the incomparable, undisputable, undefeatable boxing champion of the world. No one could defeat him as a professional boxer.

In a Biblical sense, this is true about Jesus Christ. The nails of the cross could not hold Him, the grave could not keep Him, and death could not contain Him. The Roman government could not get rid of Him, the Jews could not annihilate Him, and lies could not diminish Him. Public humiliation could not erase Him, skinning Him alive could not destroy Him, a spear wound inflicted to His side could not conquer Him. The devil in hell along with every force of evil known to humankind could not wipe Him out!

The reason for this is that grace is undefeatable!

Here is the truth about grace, it is always victorious. Grace never loses because God cannot be defeated. Therefore, the believer in the Lord Jesus Christ should always spell victory G-R-A-C-E.

The Treasure Of His Goodness

Wherefore he saith, when he ascended up on high, he led captivity captive, and gave gifts unto men, (Now that he ascended, what is it but that he also descended first into the lower parts of the earth?) He that descended is the same also that ascended up far above all heavens, that he might fill all things (4:8-10, KJV).

1. Any time nations fight and one nation is conquered, there are spoils of war. Spoils are those items that come from the camp of the enemy that you took and now own. Sometimes spoils can even be the release of hostages. In most cases, spoils are precious things like gold, silver, and costly items taken by the victorious nation and given to those people who belong to the victor.

2. With this in mind, this verse should cause you to rejoice and here is why. When Jesus Christ rose from the dead, He released what the Kingdom of hell thought it could keep and Jesus, our eternal King, brought back *"gifts unto men."* This verse should be looked upon in this manner; anything that hell had that our

Savior died for you to possess, is yours as a gift because King Jesus took it when the grave was emptied of His remains.

3. The Holy Spirit is your salvation, joy, and peace; answered prayer, healing, hope, and help are all yours! The devil had it, but Christ would not let him keep it.

4. Every time you see a cross, you should shout like you have victory. The phrase Paul uses here *"...gave gifts unto men..."* is the portrait of a man returning from battle after a fight and though he is scarred, he is victorious, and the spoils of war are in his hands. This is what Jesus looked like on Resurrection Sunday! He had the spoils of war in His hands. It is why our Redeemer declared *"...all power is given unto me in heaven and earth" (Matt. 28:18b, KJV).*

5. Never forget this, the cross was the place of battle, and King Jesus will forever be our vicarious victor!

The Triumph That He Gives

*   Floyd Mayweather will one day meet death and die. So he may have fifty wins and zero losses today, but one day he too will lose to death. How does it make you feel knowing that one day you also will die if the rapture does not occur first?

*   When you hear the words "eternal life" what comes to mind for you?

*   One of the most precious gifts that Jesus Christ gives is the gift of salvation. Have you received this gift? If so, how does it make you feel? If not, would you accept it if the Lord gave it to you today?

*   John 3:16 is a Bible verse every believer should know. Take a moment and read it. How does it make you feel to know that the life you have in Christ is "everlasting"?

*   Remember this, in Christ Jesus you are undefeatable.

A Short Talk With God

Lord of heaven, thank you for defeating death, hell and the grave for me. My soul rejoices in knowing you as both Lord of lords and King of all kings. Thank you Jesus, for being my incomparable, undisputable, undefeatable champion. All of the glory belongs to you! In your name I petition heaven, Jesus, Amen!

Day 5-Week 4
The Truth About Grace

I loved playing football as a kid. In my neighborhood growing up, we used to play football every football season. It was touch in the street and tackle in the ditch. My only problem was, I wanted to be the quarterback. No, throwing was not my gift. No, I did not have much speed (Okay, I'm too big to move fast). And, no I did not play the position well. I wanted to be the quarterback because it was the position that received most of the attention. No one knows the name of guys who block. We see the quarterback!

It was the game of the century, and I demanded to play quarterback because it was my team. I threw numerous interceptions, but I blamed it on the receivers running wrong routes. I fumbled twice, but I blamed it on the grease that was still on my hands left over from my lunch at Popeye's chicken (the three-piece campus special I had earlier that day). And, to make matters worse, we lost the game and never scored a touchdown. While sitting on the edge of a ditch sulking from my horrible performance as a QB, one of my best friends told me why we lost so horribly. He merely said, "Bobby, you're too big to be a quarterback! Play the position you are made to play. Block somebody and y'all might just win."

Often, when it relates to the work of the church on earth, people are just in the wrong spots. Folks are regularly playing the wrong position. The result is greeters who are mean as wolves that have not eaten in a week, hospitability servants who are not hospitable at all and servants that never serve anyone. Have you ever seen a church where they have good people in all the wrong places? It is a mess every time.

Here is the truth about grace; the grace of the Lord will lead you to work in the place that the Lord has ordained for you. It is best described as the place of grace.

The Treasure Of His Goodness

And he gave some, apostles; and some, prophets; and some, evangelists; and some, pastors and teachers; for the perfecting of the saints, for the work of the ministry, for the edifying of the body of Christ: till we all come in the unity of the faith, and of the knowledge of the Son of God, unto a perfect man, unto the measure of the stature of the fullness of Christ: that we henceforth be no more children, tossed to and fro, and carried about with every wind of doctrine, by the sleight of men, and cunning craftiness, whereby they lie in wait to deceive; but speaking the truth in love, may grow up into him in all things, which is the head, even Christ from whom the whole body fitly joined together and compacted by that which every joint supplied, according to the effectual working in the measure of every part, market increase of the body unto the edifying of itself in love (4:11-16, KJV).

1.   Here is the starting line up for a winning team and each position has its place in time. God gave (without fee or charge) some apostles (men hand picked by the Messiah who walked with Jesus during His earthly ministry: Matt. 10:1-4), some prophets (men and women who foretold the coming of the Messiah, death of the Messiah, the return of the Messiah and the ultimate rule of the Messiah), some evangelists (men and women called by God during the church age to declare the Gospel of Jesus Christ), and some pastors who are teachers. Notice the job of the pastor; *poimen* is to care for the flock of God as a shepherd by teaching.

2.   With this in mind, the purpose of teaching by the pastor is to *"...perfect the saints for the work of the ministry, for the edifying of the body of Christ..."* This means the pastor's job is team preparation for ministry. The word used for the term "edify" came from the discipline of brick masons in first century Judaism. It is used by experienced men who knew where to put each rock in a stonewall or each rock in a stone fence. The blessing in such a structure is that no rock is the same, and no place is the same, but each rock has a purpose. The purpose of each brick is to play its role in making the house complete.

3.   Here is the shout about this passage. Your role in God's Kingdom may not be my role, but if you just do your part, it makes every part work together in the ".... unity of the faith..." Notice that teaching should continue until the body of Christ grows up and becomes so much like Christ that we remind the world of the Christ that graced us to grow in the first place.

4.   This is very important, all too often we find that believers are ".... tossed to and fro with every wind and doctrine..." This happens because, as a Christian, if you do not know what you believe, you will believe anything. Sound doctrine matters and without it we are lost.

5.   Notice in closing, that Christ is the head and the entire body is ".... fitly joined together..." This phrase means to fasten with fire; to make parts that are joined together permanently. It is where we stand in and for the unity of Christ Jesus until time is no more. Never forget this, to be in your place and to play your part

means everything in the body of Christ. Many people sit in worship week after week but do not serve anywhere. However, God did not save you just to sit. We are a part of a body that is left here on earth to serve the one true and living God, Jesus Christ.

The Triumph That He Gives

- Imagine a beautiful brick home in your mind. Now imagine that each brick was a different shape, size, and color. This is how the Kingdom of God should look in the local church. If you have been born-again, you are a brick. Now here is the question. What role would your life play in the Kingdom of God?

- In most cases, gifted, talented and skilled believers sit on their gifts in the local church. Why do you think this happens?

- Are you using your gifts, talents, and skills to serve God in your local assembly? Why? Why not?

- Please know this, you are not serving God so that you can be saved. Salvation is a free gift. You should, however, serve God because you are saved. With this in mind, what more could you do for the Lord that you are not doing right now?

- Never forget this, there is always a bundle of excuses regarding why you may not be serving as you should. But there is only one reason that you should serve God in the church until He comes again. You should serve the Lord because you love Him so much that you have learned to serve Him by helping others (Read Col. 3:23).

A Short Talk With God

Eternal God my Father, if you could allow your only Son to die for me, I can do more for you by serving others. Lord, grow me in your Word through the teaching of my pastor and bless me so that I might be a blessing to the body of Christ on earth. In the name of your Son and my Savior, I Pray. In the name of Jesus, who is Lord and Christ, Amen.

Day 6-Week 4
The Truth About Grace

It was the fall of 1984, and I was now a freshman at Texas Southern University. I'm excited because I have been recruited to march in the greatest band in the land, the Ocean of Soul. The recruiters were so polite and kind, but when band practice started everything changed overnight. No more Mr. Nice Guy! It was out with the old and in with the new. A whole new program was about to start, and it took me by storm. They made me cut off my Jheri Curl. Can you believe that? I had to wear a white T-shirt to practice every day. I could not walk on any grass; no sodas, juices or deserts. This thing was out of control. Not to mention, I had to answer my peers like I was in the military by shouting "Yes Sir!" Practice started at five in the morning and would last until after midnight. I wanted to quit! After all, I signed up for band, not the United States Marine Corp.

To make matters worse, we traveled all of the time, and that meant taking one uniform off and putting on another one. It meant packing and continually changing. I hated it, at first, but I learned to love it. I fell so in love with it that by my junior year I was the president of this marching machine. Here is the bottom line; it was not easy because it required change. I did not have to be in the band; I wanted to be in the band. That meant sacrifice. It meant hard work. It meant dedication. It meant change!

So it is with the believer in Jesus Christ. Jesus did not die for you to remain in the state that you were in when you met Him. Salvation is free, but discipleship is costly. The one thing that you can be sure of is change is inevitable.

Here is the truth about grace; to be a follower of Jesus Christ means change. It is out with the old and in with the new. The Lord of heaven will change your life for the better. To meet Jesus Christ is to know what that change is all about.

The Treasure Of His Goodness

This I say therefore, and testify in the Lord, that ye henceforth walk not as other Gentiles walk, in the vanity of their mind, having the understanding darkened, being alienated from the life of God through the ignorance that is in them, because of the blindness of their heart: who being past feeling have given themselves over unto lasciviousness, to work all uncleanness with greediness. But ye have not so learned Christ; if so be that ye have heard him, and have been taught by him, as the truth is in Jesus: that ye put off concerning the former conversation the old man, which is corrupt according to the deceitful lusts; and be renewed in the spirit of your mind; and that ye put on the new man, which after God is created in righteousness and true holiness. Wherefore putting away lying, speaks every man truth with his neighbor: for we are members one of another. Be ye angry, and sin not: let not the sun go down upon your wrath: neither give place to the devil. Let him that stole steal no more: but rather let him labor, working with his hands the thing which is good, that he may have to give to him that needeth. Let no corrupt communication proceed out of your mouth, but that which is useful to the use of edifying, that it may minister grace unto the hearers. And grieve not the Holy Spirit of God, whereby ye are sealed unto the day of redemption. Let all bitterness, and wrath, and anger, and clamor, and evil speaking, be put away from you, with all malice: and be ye kind one to another, tenderhearted, forgiving one another, even as God for Christ's sake hath forgiven you. (4:17-32, KJV).

1. Did you read this passage? If so, read it once more. It is one of the most challenging passages in the entire Bible. To say you love Jesus Christ is one thing, but to commit to Him means out with the old and in with the new.

2. In this passage, Paul makes it clear that there are some things that following Jesus means that you should do without. Things that the "old man" loved and used to do. Okay, so this needs to be made clear here. In every believer, there is an old you and a new you. The old you is a reference to the sinful you that once sinned and had not encountered grace. The new you is the you that has tasted grace and realize that you owe God a debt that you will never be able to repay Him. Here is the challenge, take off the old and put on the new.

3. There is a great comparison and contrast given in the passage. The "old man" and the "new man" are pitted against each other. What is even deeper is that human volition is the modus operandi to making the "old man" decrease and "new man" increase. In short, we are not told to pray about the habits of the "old man," but we are told to "put it away." The language is that of a man in the market picking up fruit and can decide on what pieces of fruit he wants. The man can keep the apples but "put away" the oranges. The choice belongs to him. Likewise, Paul says, "put away" things that relate to the "old man." The choice is yours.

4. Most importantly, the backbone to the decision-making is being taught the Word of God. The more Word you are taught, the better decisions you should make every day.

5. One of the pieces of evidence that the "old man" is off and the "new man" is on is the kind of language that comes out of your mouth. There is a saying that "What is in the well of the heart, comes up in the bucket of the mouth." A better saying may be to suggest that what is on the hard drive of your laptop will eventually end up on your screen for everyone to see. Whatever the case, if you want to see which man is in charge at any point in time, monitor the language that falls from your lips.

The Triumph That He Gives

- In what ways has knowing Jesus Christ changed your life?
- Be open, honest and genuinely transparent for a moment. What are some characteristics of your "old man" that you know you need to put off?
- What are some characteristics of your "new man" that you can honestly testify that knowing Jesus Christ has changed for you?
- Read Romans 7:14-End. There are times when the "old man" gets the best of us no matter how much the "new man" grows. Has this ever happened to you?
- Remember this, God's Word feeds the "new man, " and the "old man" eats everything else. Like weeds in the garden of your life, the "old man" does not need to be fertilized or cultivated, but the "new man" does. Feed your "new man" often and the "new man" will give you the strength to put off the "old man" when test time comes.

A Short Talk With God

Lord Jesus, there are times when my "old man" gets the best of me and my "new man" struggles. In those moments, give me more grace and grant me more strength in the inner man. My heart's desire is to live for you. My soul finds refuge in you and you alone. My joy in knowing you Lord causes me to say, you have made an excellent change in my life. God please have your way with me. Take out what you don't you do not need and grow what remains. In Jesus name, Amen.

Chapter 5

At Least Try To Act Like You Belong To Me!

Week 5

<u>The Grace Of Human Harmony</u>

Day 1-Week 5
The Truth About Grace

My immediate family is a very close and clannish group. Here is how my family works, if you are in the family, you are in. If you are not in the family, you are not. Now if you are in the family, you can talk the family talk with us. But if you are not, then know that our family talk is an A and B conversation so C your way out. Catch my drift? With this in mind, allow me to let you eavesdrop on a little Adolph household right quick. My mother was a disciplinarian to her heart. She said things one time, and that was it. Her backhand had absolutely nothing to do with her ability to play tennis, and she was filled with mother-wit sayings that sounded like threats, and none of her children wanted to see if she was serious regarding them or not. She said some things all of the time that was an intricate part of her training regime.

Momma said things like, "I brought you into this world and I will take you out of here too." "You'd better act like you've got some sense before I knock some sense into you." "Did you say something? Say it loud enough for me to hear you." "You must be losing your mind." "Fix your attitude before I help you with it. And, I mean fix it right now." And, this one, "I don't care what all of the other children are doing. You represent me and this family when you go somewhere, so at least act like you belong to me!"

My mother had high standards for all of her children and she never lowered them for any of us. You were going to say "yes sir" and "no ma'am" to every adult. You were going to pick up after yourself, do what you were told to do, and for heaven's sake, you were never going to be disrespectful to any adult for any reason. It was just the rules of the house, and it was how it was going to be at all times.

Like my mother had high standards for her kids, God has even higher standards for His children. To be in God's family brings to the forefront issues of accountability and responsibility that must be addressed at all times.

Here is the truth about grace, God declares to those who are His own, at least try to act like you belong to me.

The Treasure Of His Goodness

Be ye therefore followers of God, as dear children; and walk in love, as Christ also hath loved us, and hath given himself for us an offering and a sacrifice to God for a sweetsmelling savor. But fornication, and all uncleanness, or covetousness, let it not be once named among you, as becometh saints; neither filthiness, nor foolish talking, nor jesting, which are not convenient: but rather giving of thanks. For this ye know, that no whoremonger, nor unclean person, nor covetous man, who is an idolater, hath any inheritance in the kingdom of Christ and of God (5:1-5, KJV).

1. There is one thing that makes God smile regarding His children for sure. It is when we "...walk in love, as Christ hath also loved us..." In fact, Jesus gave this to His disciples as a new commandment for them to follow and for us too '...love one another..." (John 13:34, KJV). This is both easy and hard depending on whom the recipient of your love is. It is easy to love people who are lovable. However, some folks push all of the wrong buttons and get on your last nerve. The standard is still the same for them. Love them! It is the command of our Father. Read 1 John 4:20. Now remember this, love is the family authenticator for the people of God.

2. There is a shift in this passage that must be noticed. We shift from believers loving believers to believers loving God based on our actions. In short, if we love God and accept the fact that He has given us the "...sweet smelling savor..." of His Son for our sacrifice, we should love Him back. This love should be visible in our everyday actions and activity. Therefore, "...fornication, sexual impurity,

and other deeds of the flesh..." should be done away with.

3.   Here is an excellent question to ask. Why does Paul always seem to target sexual sins all of the time? Paul does this because in the first century Judaism you could tell what god a person served by looking at what their sexual behavior was like. Sex was used to honor various so-called deities, especially those in Ephesus. So Paul targeted these fleshly actions as a way of determining what god you served. In short, a real Christian honors God by using sexual intimacy as He has ordained and instructed it to be used.

4.   In the latter segment of this passage, Paul draws a line in the sand. He stands boldly and says "...no whoremonger or unclean person...." can have an inheritance in the Kingdom. Why is this? Humanity is God's creation, but we are not all God's children. You know His children because His children do what He has told them to do.

5.   Remember this; grace is not a ticket to sin; it is a motivating factor to live holy.

The Triumph That He Gives

•   Think back to your childhood for a moment. Did you ever get into trouble for doing something that you had no business doing? What happened?

•   If you knew that it was wrong, why did you do it?

•   When you finished doing the wrong thing even though you knew it was wrong, did you still belong to your parents? Why didn't they disown you and throw you away?

•   In many ways, our human relationships with our parents are just like those that we have with God. Have you ever done exactly what God told you not to do? How did you feel? What did God do to you?

•   Keep this in mind; the love of God is so real that it makes room for His grace never to fail. If you belong to God and He is your Father then do your best to try and act like it?

A Short Talk With God

God today I am thankful that I'm not what I used to be. However, I somewhat saddened to admit to you in prayer that I not what I should be either. Lord, it is my sincere desire to please you. However, there are times when I'm trying my best to please you that I fall and falter along the way. Please, Lord, move those things from my life that are not pleasing to you. If you do not move them, give me the strength to get rid of them. I love what you love, and I hate what you hate. Thank you for the standards that you have for all of your children. Help me maintain each one of them so that when I pass from time and slip into eternity, I can hear your voice say, servant well done. In Jesus name, Amen!

FROM THE DIRECTORS CHAIR

Click or type this link into your browser to view: https://youtu.be/FAVlv-23D2A

1. Two wrongs will never make a right. What are some apparent mistakes that Dionese has made?

2. Compromise can be dangerous. It is one of the many ways believers can become ensnared by the enemy. Have you ever been entangled in a situation that you got yourself into but could not get yourself out of? What did God do for you? Did He let you taste His grace? What happened?

3. The horror of church life is found in the fact that people come to the house of God looking for Him and run into us. We can be sinful, mean, abrasive, harsh and downright evil. Why do you think God lets people run into us and not just Him?

4. It is one thing to have a past. It is another thing to live there. Do you think the pastor is living in his past? What about Dionese? What about you?

5. One of the significant failures of Christians today the world over is our failure to model for the world what Jesus Christ is really like. In what ways does Dionese fail at doing this? In what ways can every Christian in the kingdom of God do a better job of this for the sake of Christ?

Day 2-Week 5
The Truth About Grace

It was pure deception, I just did not know it at the time. Okay, here is what went down. It was senior skip day. My friend Michael Cole told me it was legal for us to miss class that day, so I did. He had been my friend for years, and I should have noticed that little devilish smirk on his face, but I let it go. I loaded up my Pontiac Bonneville and headed for the park. That is where the party was supposed to be. The only problem was that somebody forgot to tell the other students. No one was there but my car full, leaping fish in the lake, birds tweeting in the trees and a few passers-by looking at us like, "Hey shouldn't you guys be in school?" Wait I forgot to mention that I was not a senior. That hit me like a ton of bricks when a Truant Officer, who told all of us that we were in hot water, stopped us. Of course, I was driving, it was my car, and I took the whole blame.

I looked at Michael and said, "dude why did you lie to me?" He smirked and said, "Big John, the devil made me do it." I wanted to choke him! My parents took my car from me. I was back riding old yellow. Just in case you're unfamiliar with that terminology, it is a reference to a school bus. My girlfriend dumped me because she wanted a man with a car. My popularity sank like the Titanic, and all I had to show for it was a busted trip to an empty park with a car full of knuckleheads.

Here is the truth about grace, once you know better, you have a moral obligation to do better or at least try. So no matter what anyone tells you to do, stick to what you know is right and leave wrong alone. Hold fast to the truth and live it with all that you've got.

The Treasure Of His Goodness

Let no man deceive you with vain words: for because of these things cometh the wrath of God upon the children of disobedience. Be not ye therefore partakers with them. For ye were sometimes darkness, but now are ye light in the Lord: walk as children of light: (For the fruit of the Spirit is in all goodness and righteousness and truth;) proving what is acceptable unto the Lord (5:6-10, KJV).

1. We are living in the age of deception. The word "deceive" used in this passage means to trick for the purpose of treachery. It was used for a fisherman's net that would entrap fish that would later be used for dinner. Deception is most hurtful

because it is not always obvious. More than that, it is something that comes from nearby proximity.

2. This is why you want a preacher who will tell you the truth no matter what. If your preacher lies to you and deceives you, the punishment is still the same.

3. Deception and compromise are two sides of the same coin. There are times that we know better, but we try to compromise it. The result is ruin.

4. This passage challenges believers in Christ to "...walk as Children of light..." How do you know when you are walking in the light? "...The fruit of the spirit..." becomes manifest in your life. Most importantly, what God approves of becomes what you stand for both in public and in private.

5. Keep this in mind; our enemy is a deceiver. He lures believers into sin all of the time by using lies and compromise.

The Triumph That He Gives

- Have you ever been deceived? What took place? What happened?

- There are times that we know right from wrong and chose poorly. This happens when we compromise Christian virtues or lie to ourselves regarding the truth. Has this ever happened to you?

- The phrase "...children of disobedience..." is used here to reference people who live in disobedience rather than honoring God. Have you ever had a season of your life where you lived in disobedience? What changed you?

- No fruit grows on a tree without having great roots that produce it. The same principle carries over into our spiritual walk. If you want to know how your spiritual walk with God is going, take a moment and examine your fruit. Paul says the fruit of the spirit is in all "...goodness, righteousness and truth..." Take a moment and look at your life. What fruit do you see?

- Keep this in mind; God never cuts a tree of His down. He always gives it another chance to grow. Read St. Mark Luke 13:6-19 and John 15:1-6.

A Short Talk With God

Lord of heaven and earth I want to live for you more now than ever before. My heart desires to please you, yet there have been moments and times when I have been deceived. I had moments of personal compromise and times when my spiritual fruit was not its best. But you graciously gave me another chance. Thank you for loving me when I was not lovable and being merciful to me when I did not deserve any mercy at all. I love you and bless you for who you are in my life. In the name of Jesus, I petition heaven. Amen!

Day 3-Week 5
The Truth About Grace

Have you ever heard the adage that birds of a feather flock together? It is not true all of the time. But, it is true much of the time. Not long ago, I attended an AA meeting to celebrate with a member of the church who was being awarded a twenty-five year chip for sobriety. As I listened to the testimonies that came from the people present, I found the story of Jason most compelling. Jason addressed the group in standard AA like fashion by saying, "Hi, I'm Jason, and I'm a no good addict." To which the entire group responded in antiphonal like fashion, "Hi, Jason." He then proceeded to tell them about a relapse that he suffered and what caused it years ago. He told the group that he thought that he could maintain relationships with friends who still used drugs but just being near them caused his demise. Jason said, "When I stopped walking with people of darkness, I found walking in the light much easier to do."

Here is the fundamental truth, who you are with will not only define you, but they can confine you as well. The company you keep can either keep you or curse you. The choice is yours.

Here is the truth about grace, God gives you your parents and family but allows you to chose your friends. Choose well because you will soon become what you affiliate yourself with.

The Treasure Of His Goodness

And have no fellowship with the unfruitful works of darkness, but rather reprove them. For it is a shame even to speak of those things which are done of them in secret. But all things that are reproved are made manifest by the light: for whatsoever doth make manifest is light. Wherefore he saith, Awake thou that sleepest, and arise from the dead, and Christ shall give thee light. See then that ye walk circumspectly, not as fools, but as wise, redeeming the time, because the days are evil. Wherefore be ye not unwise, but understanding what the will of the Lord is (5:11-17, KJV).

1. Listen, if you are connected to people who will pull you backwards, take you downwards or help you to sin, cut them off and run away from them. Paul tells the church in Ephesus like this, "...Have no fellowship with the unfruitful works

of darkness..." It is interesting to note, that when you are connected with people who are in darkness, their work is unfruitful. Yes, it could be profitable. But, all money is not good money. The reason Paul calls it "unfruitful" is because a lifestyle that dwells in the dark cannot ever make the God who is both light and life happy. Paul says that we should reprove them. This means to speak ill towards something that should not be accepted. In fact, it should be looked upon as a disgrace. The prefix "dis" means to be without and the root word grace means God's favor. So a disgrace is someone who tries to function without the favor of God in their lives.

2. Notice that Paul uses two extremes in this passage to compare and contrast good works and sinful behavior. Actions that are sinful are those things that are connected to that which is involved in darkness, and the works of the Lord are those works that include the light. Therefore, whenever you shine a light, it "reproves" that which is dark. This is why Jesus, in His sermon on the mount, declared that believers should be the ".... light of the world..." (Mat. 5:14, KJV). In short, to reprove a sin is to cast light on a dark spot.

3. Paul uses the words "awake" as it pertains to sleep and "arise" as it relates to being resurrected. This is very rich in significance. The Greek use for "awake" means to rise from slumber, but the term "arise," suggest standing up after being knocked down for a good while. Paul says, "awake" to people who are reading a letter. So we know he is not referring to physical sleep here. Paul is saying pay attention to what is going on around you and "arise" or better said, take a stand and do not act like you are dead and unable to do so.

4. In our day and time, people are looking for something real. Nothing is more redemptively real than a Christian who walks the walk and puts grace on display each day. It is the charge that Paul gives when he says, "...walk circumspectly..." and not as someone who does not know better. Walk as someone who is not walking in the dark with no light, but walk in the light and it does away with the darkness.

5. Keep this in mind; darkness is not just the opposite of light, it is the absence of it. If you ever want to get rid of the dark, just turn on the light.

The Triumph That He Gives

- Have you ever had a sin friend who was always up to no good?

- When you were near them, who ended up winning the battle between the light that you carry for Christ and the darkness that they bring to the table?

- There is a difference between staying connected to your old friends to win them to Jesus Christ with your lifestyle and hanging out with them and indulging in the things that they do. Have you ever tried to win some of your lost friends or family members but got lost in sin in the process?

- Walking right is a moral and spiritual obligation that we have to God as believers in Jesus Christ. However, there are always parts of our lives that are "not quite right." How do you balance the two?

- Paul concludes this passage with a phrase that demands our attention. He says, "...understanding what the will of the Lord is." What do you think the "will of the Lord is" for your life? If you want an excellent Biblical view of the answer, use this passage as your answer sheet and go back and reread the entire passage.

A Short Talk With God

Father in heaven please guide, guard and govern my life as it relates to the company that I keep. Build a fence all around me and keep people away from me who mean me no earthly good. It is my prayer before heaven and earth to walk the walk of a believer in Jesus Christ without error or mishap. Order my steps so that the life I live is one that honors you. And on the days that I fall, falter or fail do not let me utterly be destroyed, for your Word says you will " ...uphold me with your hand" (Psalms 37:24b). In the name of Jesus Christ, Amen.

Day 4-Week 5
The Truth About Grace

For the second time in major league baseball history, the Houston Astros made it to the World Series. The city of Houston was buzzing with excitement. I priced some of the tickets to the big game and suddenly remembered that I was not rich as of yet. Just to stand in the stadium and watch the game on a screen costs $800.00. Needless to say, I watched the game in the comfort of my home, in my easy chair with my feet propped up hoping for a championship. It would be Houston's first!

The Astros did not just land accidentally in the big game. They have had sizzling bats and great pitching all year long. Earlier in the season, I took my son to a game when tickets were $49.00 to sit on the first base line (can you tell that I'm cheap.... don't judge me) and the 'Stros won. Walking out the stadium we encountered a fan that just had one too many. He was not only tipsy, he was tight. He was not merely semi-inebriated, he was completely intoxicated. Okay, let me just say it, he was drunk.

He hugged everyone with an Astros jersey on, fell twice and never spilled one drop of his beer. I overheard a kid ask his dad "What is wrong with that guy?" His father (wearing his church t-shirt and an Astros cap) said, "He is full of spirits. It is just not the Holy Spirit, that's for sure."

Make no mistake about it; alcohol alters the mental state every time. It is the leading form of addiction in America. It is delightful to many but dangerous to all. It is why Paul admonishes the Ephesian Church not to be full of alcohol.

Here is the truth about grace, if you are going to be full of anything, empty yourself of you and fill yourself with God's spirit. The bar is open, the tab is paid, and refills are on the house.

The Treasure Of His Goodness

And be not drunk with wine, wherein is excess; but be filled with the Spirit; speaking to yourselves in psalms and hymns and spiritual songs, singing and making melody in your heart to the Lord; giving thanks always for all things unto God and the Father in the name of our Lord Jesus Christ; submitting yourselves one to another in the fear of God (5:18-21, KJV).

1. The warning about wine in this passage comes because alcohol, during the first century Judaism, was used to intoxicate cultic prostitutes before the god, Bacchus, so they would be filled with his spirit of seduction. Paul pushes the church to run from alcohol because of its addictive properties.

2. The contrast in the text is not just to run from alcohol but also to be filled with the Spirit. It is important to note that you cannot be filled with anything until you are first empty of yourself. What is not mentioned is how you get filled with the Spirit. A simple answer would be to ask God for more of His presence in your life (Matt. 7:7).

3. This is very important to remember. In chapter one of this letter, Paul tells us about the sealing of the Spirit (1:13-14) and now he is charging the church regarding being filled with the spirit (5:18). These are two different happenings. As a believer in Jesus Christ, you are sealed with the spirit once and for all. However, as a Christian, there are times that you need to be filled over and over again. The sealing of the spirit is redemptive and permanent, but the filling of the spirit is reoccurring.

4. Notice that once you are filled, you can speak to others. This is so deep. This is not to slight anyone's interpretation of this passage, but a person, who is filled with the spirit, doesn't just talk in unknown tongues; they can speak to people kindly. In fact, the way they speak is so kind, it makes music in the human heart and pleases God.

5. Most importantly, a spiritually filled believer is a thankful Christian. The words "giving thanks" used by Paul comes from the Greek term ***eucharisteo***, and it means to boast on grace. Here is how it works, the Holy Spirit within you reminds you of the grace that has come to you and bragging about God's goodness joyfully comes from you. In short, the more grace you receive, the more gratitude you should produce.

The Triumph That He Gives

*   Do you drink alcohol? If so, have you ever been intoxicated? What happened to you if you can recall?

- When was the last time you earnestly ask God to fill you again with His presence?

- Have you ever encountered at least one person who you just refused to speak to or talk to? Who are they? What did they do to you?

- Has it ever occurred to you that the reason you are unable to speak to them is that you are too full yourself? Keep in mind; believers who are filled with God's spirit can talk to anyone.

- Remember this; a Spirit-filled life is merely a life lived in total submission to God. The imminent presence of the Lord within you causes you to serve the God who remains transcendent above you.

A Short Talk With God

Jesus, I want more of you in my life. I need more of you in my life. I desire more of you in my life. If I could ask you for anything right now, it would not be for anything other than more you. Fill me again with your spirit and cause me to be a living example of your redemptive love. Thank you for filling me again. I earnestly needed it. In your name, I pray, Amen.

Day 5-Week 5
The Truth About Grace

Just because you see a person standing on the golf course does not mean that they can play golf. Golf requires a specific set of skills that can take a lifetime to develop. Just because you see a man sitting on a piano stool with a baby grand piano in front of him does not mean he can play the piano. He may not be able to find middle C with a flashlight and a pair of binoculars. Here is the point; some things in life require skill to function well.

I see people get married all of the time. In fact, I will average about seventy weddings a year. Of those marriages, most of the brides have no idea what it will take to be a wife. Of course, we offer training classes at the church. And, those brides-to-be sit through those sessions with their eyes wide shut. Their minds are on flowers, dresses, colors, programs, dinner selections and most importantly, the wedding dress. They get married, and when the reality of being attached to Fred Flintstone sets in, they come running out of that house like Wilma Flintstone, with Pebbles on one hip and Bam-Bam on the other seeking emergency counsel and refuge from Betty Rubble living next door. In short, the whole thing ends up in a mess.

Let's set the record straight, being a wife is no easy task. You have to know when to talk, when to listen, when to pray, when to go easy and when to put your foot down. It is a skill set.

Here is the truth about grace; God gave us human relationships on earth so that people on earth would treasure a heavenly relationship with God through His Son, Jesus Christ. No other relational institution does that like marriage does.

The Treasure Of His Goodness

Wives, submit yourselves unto your own husbands, as unto the Lord. For the husband is the head of the wife, even as Christ is the head of the church: and he is the savior of the body. Therefore as the church is subject unto Christ, so let the wives be to their own husbands in everything (5:22-24, KJV).

1. The passage opens with the word "wives." Please know that a wife is not only a woman with a husband, but she is also a woman who deserves to have one. In short, she can handle him and has the skill to deal with him. Read Proverbs 31:10-end. Notice the virtuous woman mentioned in that passage does not need

a man to make her who she is. She qualifies to have a man because she will soon define him.

2. Now for the hard part. A wife is to "submit" herself to her husband. The Greek word Paul uses here is **hupatasso** it reminds you of a hot potato because that is what you will get if you try to make a woman do anything against her wishes. The term means to place under the authority of another. It was a military term used to denote rank. So here is how it works, a wife willingly accepts the fact that her husband is a higher-ranking figure in the order of God and voluntarily yields to his authority.

3. It should not go without mention here that in the military, rank is recognized based on mandatory standards. In short, a private first class will salute a three-star general. Why? It is mandatory. However, in marital relationships rank is not recognized on mandatory standards, but voluntary decisions. This is precisely seen every time a husband tries to make his wife do something, and she says, "take a hike buster!" In marriage, a wife is to be won by submission.

4. It is clear that the husband is the head. Not the wife. To have a wife as the head destroys the model set forth here in the passage. It should also not go without mentioning that there are not two heads. Just one. Also, it is worthy of note that before there can be the submission of the wife to the husband, there must be a mutual submission of both the husband and the wife to God. Read Ephesians 5:21 again.

5. This is one of the most abused verses in the Bible. Angry husbands grab the Bible and point to it when they have it out with their wives regarding their duties as a wife. But keep this in mind, her submission is not mandatory, it is voluntary. She only submits for two reasons. She loves God enough to do it, and she loves her husband enough to grant it graciously.

The Triumph That He Gives

*   Have you ever met a wife who made you look at her and say, "She is awesome"? Who was she?

*   What qualities made you admire her?

*   How did she treat her husband?

- Do you think she was the kind of woman who could keep a family together?

- Never forget this, a real wife not only knows how to deal with her husband she is the glue that keeps a family together.

A Short Talk With God

God lay your hand on every woman who is a wife right now and bless her with the patience, strength, fortitude, and ability to keep her family together. In Jesus' name. Amen.

Day 6-Week 5
The Truth About Grace

I will never forget this as long as I live. I was at a picnic and bar-b-que was piled a mile high. Potato salad, green beans, rice dressing, boudin, ribs, brisket and peach cobbler were sitting all around us. When it was time to eat, it was like every man for himself. But, an older man was sitting in his lawn chair just relaxing in the shade. Of course, all of the guys with us were kind and mannerable, so they let the ladies eat first. But the old man wasn't moving. After waiting in line to load our plates, we took notice of a gorgeous older lady who was preparing two plates at one time. When she reached the end of the line, she walked over to the old man in the lawn chair, handed him his plate, put her hand on her hip and said, "Henry is that all you want?" He said, "Yeah Baby." Without any hesitation, all of the young married men pulled our lawn chairs next to his.

One young man said, "How did you train your wife to do that?" You see none of our wives fixed our plates. We were like scavengers looking for what we could find. The old man looked at all of us young husbands and said "Yall don't know what you doing with a woman. She's like a field that you till that will give you fruit if you know how to work it. Plant good seeds and you will always get good things. Sow bad seeds, and you will never get fruit, and you will have to learn to live with weeds."

We sat listening to him for hours. When this old man finished, we all knew at least one thing, just because we were married did not make us a husband. We needed lessons on how to treat a wife and we needed them right away.

Here is the truth about grace, just like Christ has loved you into submission, so should a husband treat his wife in the same manner.

The Treasure Of His Goodness

Husbands, love your wives, even as Christ also loved the church, and gave himself for it; that he might sanctify and cleanse it with the washing of water by the word, that he might present it to himself a glorious church, not having spot, or wrinkle, or any such thing; but that it should be holy and without blemish. So ought men to love their wives as their own bodies. He that loveth his wife loveth himself. For no man ever yet hated his own flesh; but nourisheth and cherisheth it, even as the Lord the church: for we are members of his body, of his flesh, and of his bones. For this cause shall a man leave his father and mother, and shall be joined unto his wife, and they two shall be one flesh. This is a great mystery: but I speak concerning Christ and the church. Nevertheless let every one of you in particular so love his wife even as himself; and the wife see that she reverence her husband (5:25-33, KJV).

1. Every man with a wife is not a husband. A husband is a man who qualifies to have one and knows how to take care of her. Now here is something that must be mentioned here. A husband only has one job to do to please God in a covenant relationship with his wife. He is told to "...love his wife..." that is it. Nothing more and nothing less.

2. Marriages fail every day because husbands cannot love their wives. The command that comes from the Lord is for a husband to do for his wife, what Jesus Christ has done for the church. Therefore, a husband is to love his way to the extent that Christ loved the church. Biblically speaking a married man cannot divorce his wife unless he is willing to be nailed to a tree alive in public and left for dead.

3. With this in mind, love is not how a husband should feel about his wife. Though a husband should have feelings for his wife, his love cannot be a feeling only. Why? Feelings change like the weather. In fact, it is possible for a husband to love his wife and not like her at the time. This happens because love and like are both four letter words, but they do not mean the same thing.

4. The love of a husband is an internal decision that is based on eternal truth, which is confirmed with an external covenant that carries with it a paternal promise that should last forever.

5. If a husband does not love his God and himself, he will never love his wife. In fact, if a husband fails at loving his wife, the marriage is in troubled water. But, if he loves her, it can last forever.

The Triumph That He Gives

- Wives are nothing more than sinners who are saved by grace. In short, she is not a perfect person which means sometimes she is not loveable at all. According to the lesson, how does a husband love her then?

- To love in marriage is to make a decision. Have you ever made a decision and later changed your mind? What took place?

- The blessing in the world is being married. However, with every blessing comes a burden attached. What do you think the biggest burden of Christian marriage is today?

- Husbands are never told to make their wives happy. What do you think the reason for this could be?

- The only institution in the world designed by God to show the world Christ and the church is the union of marriage between a man and a woman. Today this model of marriage is terribly under attack. Why do you think this is taking place?

A Short Talk With God

O God I lift every Christian husband to you right now, and I humbly ask for you to place in his heart a love for his wife that will never leave him alone. Lord cause husbands to love their wives unconditionally so that Christ might be exalted, marriages might endure, and families might persevere, and children might be blessed because of a husband's obedience. In Jesus name, Amen.

Chapter 6

Programs Are Good, But Parents Are Better!

Week 6
<u>The Grace Of Our Victory</u>

Day 1-Week 6
The Truth About Grace

To have a mother in your life is a gift from God. To have a father in your life is a blessing from heaven. To have both a mother and father share in your rearing is God's favor functioning in your life. It's 8310 Homewood Lane. What is this address you ask? It is the place where I was raised. My father was a pastor, a truck driver for a pharmaceutical company called McKesson and Drugs, and a part-time handyman who could fix just about anything with his hands if he wanted to. My mother was a skilled church pianist, a highly trained domestician, a non-degreed child psychologist (by this I mean she knew when you needed prayer, counseling, encouragement or a checkup from the neck up), a culinary expert, an Avon Sales Consultant (to this day I still love the smell of Skin So Soft because of my indulgence in Avon products because of her), and an entrepreneur where she owned and operated To Love A Rose Floral Company. I did not like the flower shop much because it was possible to wake up and find a casket spray sitting on the kitchen table. So there were times I did not know whether to pray for the deceased or just bless my bowl of Corn Flakes. Can you feel me?

No matter what the case was, all of my life I was blessed and favored to be reared in a two-parent household. It was far from perfect. We had our problems, issues, setbacks, heartaches, struggles, and failures, but we were a family and with God's help, we made it.

Funny thing is everything I learned about life and living came from my parents early on. I learned about Jesus Christ from my parents. I learned about respect from my parents. I learned diligence from my parents. I learned about endurance from my parents. I learned survival from my parents. I even learned about prayer from my parents. By fourteen years old, I could drive an automobile, and I am talking about a four in the floor standard shift truck that you could push start if you could get it to the top of a hill and pop the clutch. By the age of sixteen, I was a tenth-grade student and a full-time employee at Burger King making a whopping $3.35 an hour. I thought I was rich! And, by the age of eighteen years of age, I was grown and gone from my parents' house.

Today both of my parents sleep with the elders, resting upon the lap of God with their bodies planted in the couch of nature's bosom awaiting the precise sound of the trumpet in the rapture. When I reflect on all that they gave me and did for me, my soul weeps for joy. I know that I owe them something that I could never repay them. When I look back over my life, I have no recollection of being a part of a program. By this I mean, I did not need a mentoring program. God blessed me with parents. I have never been to an esteem-building program for youth. Why? I had parents. They did all of my esteem building. I had never seen a time when I had to attend a Big Brothers or Big Sisters meeting. Why? I had big brothers and a big sister at home.

Not long ago, while attending a funeral service of my friend's dad, I heard him say something that stuck with me. He said, "People came up with programs to address concerns God placed parents in your life to take care of. Don't get me wrong, programs are good, but to have parents is far better."

Here is the truth about grace, God graced you with parents and many parents have been blessed with children. It makes up the institution we call family. When family functions like God designed it to function, we must conclude that the grace of a family is far better than any of the best programs that have ever existed.

The Treasure Of His Goodness

Children, obey your parents in the Lord: for this is right. Honour thy father and mother; (which is the first commandment with promise;) that it may be well with thee, and thou mayest live long on the earth. And, ye fathers, provoke not your children to wrath: but bring them up in the nurture and admonition of the Lord (6:1-3, KJV).

1. Paul concluded chapter five by dealing intricately with the marital construct between a husband and a wife. The great Apostle stays under the roof of a family and now makes his focus in the passage children. People often say that children are different these days. However, I beg to differ. Kids are still just kids. Parents are different these days. Paul makes it very clear that children have one job description in a household. They are to obey. That's it. You see, I love the circus. To see all of those tricks they can do with animals is a marvel to me. They can get a vicious lion to lie down like a tiny cat. They can get a giant elephant to stand on one leg and lift his trunk in the air. But, we cannot get children to sit down and be quiet. Something is wrong with this picture. This is because you cannot train children on a part-time basis. It takes time. To obey your parents is the command, but obedience comes from training and training takes time.

2. When Paul mentions "...Honoring thy father and mother..." he brings us to the Ten Commandments or what is called the Decalogue. This is not a Pauline suggestion; this is a command from God. It comes with a blessing attached to it. The promise of parental honor is to live long upon the earth. It should be noted that this promise is a general guideline and not a guarantee. Most importantly, to honor simply means to appreciate for a job well done. Okay, this will be a struggle for some people, because many were abused by parents, forsaken by parents and even wounded by parents. But remember this one positive note and it will help you to honor them. Both your mother and your father did their job well by getting you here! Your presence necessitates that you honor them both.

3. A father's role in a child's life is critical. In fact, God allows a father on earth to bear the same title he carries in heaven as we call God our Father. Paul warns the Ephesian church fathers not to make their children angry or "....provoke them to wrath..." A better translation would be to say do not wear them down and be so harsh that you hinder what they could become and not help them to become all that God created them to be. Fatherhood on earth should mirror Fatherhood in heaven. No earthly father is perfect. However, with all of the imperfections a father could possess he should be an ever-present person, a priest for his home, a provider for those that are under his authority, a prayer warrior and a protector of what the Lord has given to him.

4. Keep this in mind, children will learn about God from you. So Paul presses the issue here by saying that a father should raise their children in the

"...admonition of the Lord..." The term admonition here used by Paul means to both reproof and correct. In short, fathers on earth should teach and train their children to serve God who is their Father in heaven with a noble sense of fear and reverence.

5.   Today we have many single-parent households that are being governed by women, and they are my heroes in the faith. To be both mother and father is commendable to the highest degree. In many instances, we have instituted programs to take the place of missing fathers or even fathers who are just not functioning responsibly. Please know this, no program created by people will ever replace the potency of a father who is willing to do his job and care for his children. Remember this, programs are good, but parents are better.

The Triumph That He Gives

*   Take a moment and think about the Father that God gave you. What is your recollection of your father?

*   When it regards child rearing, have you noticed how rebellious children can be these days? Why do you think this is the case?

*   Are you old enough to remember the time when switches were legal, bruises on a child's backside were permissible, parents did not abuse their kids, but raised them, and any trusted adult could chastise a child? If those days worked to produce obedient children why do you think we have forsaken this model of rearing children?

*   There are times a father can frustrate a child or even cause a child to become discouraged. Have you ever had a moment when your father caused you to become discouraged? If so, hold this truth to your heart; a human father is far from flawless. Pray for his flaws and be determined not to repeat them with your children. Learn the lesson that it taught, leave the pain that it brought.

*   Remember this, the most precious gift a father can ever give a child is a gift of knowing Jesus Christ.

A Short Talk With God

Eternal God in heaven thank you for the gift of fatherhood and the blessing of children. I pause now in my prayer time with you to ask your blessings upon all fathers. Lord strengthen those men that are doing their best and lift those fathers who have fallen by the wayside. Take your mighty hand and allow it to rest upon dads, granddads, and men who are caring for children in a way that is pleasing to you. God, our children, need you as well. Help us to reach them with your love, teach them your ideas and lead them, as they should be lead. Lord, I cannot conclude this sacred petition without asking you to be with single parents right now. Be their strength and portion. Meet their every need. In the name of Jesus, Amen.

FROM THE DIRECTORS CHAIR

Click or type this link into your browser to view: https://youtu.be?OapHZCTYMjQ

1. Demonic attack is often subtle, sneaky and covert. In what ways do you see people in the film dealing with attacks?

2. Standing in times that are tough is made for the strong. Dioneses' mother was strong. We know that because she told Dionese the truth. When dealing with spiritual warfare what role does truth play?

3. All healing comes from the Lord. In what ways did you see healing take place in the life of Dionese?

4. The enemy almost pushed Dionese to make a huge mistake. What was it? Have you ever made a huge mistake before? How did God help you deal with it?

5. To be spiritually prepared for battle causes you to be ready when the enemy strikes. The enemy hit Dionese's family years ago, and they struggled with dealing with what took place. God through His grace brought healing to her family. Do you think that He could do the same for yours? If you answered yes, you should pray right now to the Lord and ask Him for healing and restoration for any family or personal matter in your life that you cannot fix.

Day 2-Week 6
The Truth About Grace

When the alarm clock rings in the morning, it means one thing to most Americans. Get up and go to work! It says it's time to grind. Let's set the record straight; hard work is something that comes with the territory. I was always taught that no one owes you anything. If you want it, then get up and work to earn it. Work. It is the fundamental tenant of every economic system time has ever seen. Work. It is what happens when you start with nothing, conclude with something and then thank God for the something that He graced you to have. Work. People do it every day.

One of the worse work experiences I have ever had in my life came while working for the Harrison County Housing Department in the payroll department (wait, did I just put them on blast…. that was not my intent). I showed up on time every day, dressed professionally and did my job. In fact, I did whatever was needed in the office to make things work for the better. After all, I hate conflict, and I'm kind of like Rodney King. I just want all of us to get along. However, I had a supervisor who just did not care for me. For the sake of anonymity, I will call her Susie Que. Each morning I would show up, and she would be standing near the door waiting for my arrival. I was on time every time. Instead of saying good morning, she just turned and walked away as if to say "Darn he's on time again." She would often invite the accounting staff to share lunch with her and no matter what I chose for my entre, Mrs. Susie Que had something to say. On one occasion I chose grilled fish and broccoli. She said and I quote, "Mr. Adolph if you looked like your plate you would be the picture of health." Okay, I feel the need to say this for transparency. I wanted to tell her, if you had looked in the mirror carefully before leaving home, you could have gotten that matter out of your left eye. But the Lord made me hold my peace. Has God ever done that to you before?

After just eight short months of hell on earth, I was released from duty. The reason for my release was a sudden decrease in the budget. When I walked out of that door, my blood pressure became normal. My stress level dropped. My eyes went from being bloodshot red to pearly white and clear.

Here is the truth about grace, to have a good job is a blessing from the Lord so do not be found complaining about it. Be thankful for your place of employment and do your job well.

The Treasure Of His Goodness

Servants, be obedient to them that are your masters according to the flesh, with fear and trembling, in singleness of your heart, as unto Christ; not with eyeservice, as menpleasers; but as the servants of Christ, doing the will of God from the heart; with good will doing service, as to the Lord, and not to men: knowing that whatsoever good thing any man doeth, the same shall he receive of the Lord, whether he be bond or free. ⁹ And, ye masters, do the same things unto them, forbearing threatening: knowing that your Master also is in heaven; neither is there respect of persons with him (6:5-9, KJV).

1. For many years this passage was used to validate slavery in America. Slave owners would impress upon the minds of slaves that they were supposed to obey their masters. However, the word for servant used here would much better reference a person who yields their energy, effort, and labor to another for compensation. We call such people in our culture employees. Go back and re-read the passage, but put "employee" in the place where "servants" is located.

2. With this in mind, an employee should obey their employers with a degree of respect. Paul uses these terms, he calls it ".... fear and trembling..." He also says that an employee should serve with "...singleness of heart..." by this, he means that you should not show up for work every day looking for a way to hurry up and get out of your responsibilities. Do what you are paid to do.

3. Okay, let's clear the air. Some employees are horrible. They steal company supplies; spend no time doing work and a great deal of time doing absolutely nothing. To make matters worse, when a supervisor says something to a person like this, their attitude flares up and things often go awry. However, this should not be the case, people on your job should know that you love Jesus, just like the people that attend church with you do. In short, take the Lord with you to work every day. In some environments, you need Jesus just to make it through the day.

4. Paul even cautions supervisors or "master's." He says stop abusing your authority. Managers and supervisors often have the power to hire and fire. So in many instances, we have corporate bullying going on. Paul admonishes people with authority to use it in a godly way.

5. Keep this in mind, if you have a job, do your job and do it well. In fact, do it like the Lord in heaven has blessed you with it. Bearing in mind, that your job is a resource and not the source. When God gets ready to promote you, He knows just what to do and how to do it.

The Triumph That He Gives

*   Look back at your work environments you have had in the past. What was the best experience you have ever had? What was the worse experience you have ever had?

*   Be honest. What kind of employee were you? Did you work hard? Were you on time? Did you steal company time by being non-productive at work?

*   If you are employed right now take a moment and honestly rank your service to the company you are employed with. On a scale of 1 to 10, with 10 being the highest rank what kind of employee do you see yourself as being? Wait before you answer this question grab a copy of your Job Description. If you do not have one, ask your supervisor for one. Now compare what you do every day to what you were hired to do. How do you fare?

*   Supervisors can be tough. Are you are a supervisor? What kind of boss are you? If you are not a supervisor, what kind of supervisor would you be if you were one?

*   The most important thing about employer/employee relations is this, do your job as if God were watching because He is.

A Short Talk With God

Lord, you have blessed me in so many ways. One of the many ways you have shown your kindness to me is to open doors of opportunity to work and earn a living. Thank you for every door that you have ever provided for me. My prayer right now to you O God is for you to grant me your favor in my workplace. Make me proper and cause me to bloom where I am planted. Thank you for both increases and overflows. In your Son's name, Jesus I pray, amen!

Day 3-Week 6
The Truth About Grace

I have always been a fan of wrestling. Yes, I am aware that the fight is not always real. But, I just love watching it. When I was growing up in Houston, there were men like Andre the Giant and the Punisher. They would climb into the ring with enough swagger to choke a mule and fight to the finish. On one occasion I talked my father into taking me to see the matches live downtown in the Coliseum. Paul Bosh was the ringside announcer, and I was too excited.

That night Bosh announced that a new wrestler would be making his appearance. The crowd stood up in a hush and looked. They dimmed the lights and in walked this huge man who called himself the Claw. He wore a black glove on his left hand and a red cape on his back. He had on a black mask with red dots all over it that looked like drops of blood. When Paul Bosh asked him about his fight strategy in the ring, he growled and said nothing. Instead of talking, he lifted his left hand and showed the crowd the black glove. Everyone said "Oooouuuuuuu!"

The bell rang, and the fight was on. His opponent was flipping him all over the ring. We were laughing at this new guy. He was getting hammered. All of a sudden the Claw grabbed this guy in the back with his glove, and it paralyzed him for a moment. The dude got away and started running around the ring from this new wrestler. The Claw then grabbed him under his armpit, and the man shook like he was being shocked with electric voltage hot enough to light up the north side of town. He passed out in the ring. The referee counted to three and the bout was over.

When I think about the devil, I think about the Claw. He will just paw at you until something works well enough to leave you down for the count.

Here is the truth about grace, our enemy is not wearing a red cape and a black glove, but he is relentless in his pursuit to destroy us. The blessing is that our God has provided spiritual armor for believers to use that when worn we come out victorious every time.

The Treasure Of His Goodness

Finally, my brethren, be strong in the Lord, and in the power of his might. Put on the whole armor of God, that ye may be able to stand against the wiles of the devil (6:10-11, KJV).

1. The spiritual battle is inevitable for the child of God. If you are a Christian, you are involved in spiritual combat whether you are aware of it or not. Paul provides for us the most extended list of spiritual instruction given in the Bible regarding spiritual warfare.

2. In the opening verses of this text, we learn several things. We learn that the audience Paul is addressing is Christians who have made up their minds that they are going to serve the Lord, for Paul calls them "...my brethren..." We also know that Paul tells them to be "...strong in the Lord and in the power of His might..." This is very powerful here. The Greek word he uses means to use the strength of another. This is why the phrase is attached to the Lord. As believers we do not use our strength to deal with the devil, we use the Lord's strength. Our strength fades, but His strength never does get weak. Our God is strong all of the time, so we use His strength and not ours.

3. The word power in the Greek is **Kratos**, and it is power granted to another for use. Most importantly, **Kratos** comes with matters of jurisdiction attached. Therefore, this power is like that of a police officer in a city who has been given the authority to act on behalf of the chief to stop traffic, arrest criminals and the like. When God looks at you for spiritual combat, He sees one that He has given His power to. Are you rejoicing yet? You should be and here is why, it is the not the size of the officer that matters, it is the authority of the one behind the badge that counts.

4. The only way to deal with the enemy that we face is to be prepared for spiritual battle by getting dressed for the battle that we must fight. Therefore, Paul urges the Christian to "...put on the whole armor of God..."

5. Notice why we are to get dressed. It is not so that we can fight; it is so we can stand. In this passage, we are to stand against the "wiles" of the devil. The word "wiles" is most interesting. It comes from the Greek term **methodia**. It is where we borrow our methods. This provides helpful insight as to the type of attacks the enemy launches at us. The devil does not just use anything, he is strategic and specific. The devil uses various methods against us. Like the Claw, he keeps trying things until something works. This is why the whole armor is necessary for the believer to stand.

The Triumph That He Gives

- When I was younger, I thought the devil looked like the Claw. In your mind's eye, what does the enemy look like to you?

- Keep this in mind, if you can see your enemy you have the wrong enemy in mind. The word devil is *diabolos,* and he is a spirit that confuses. Therefore, wherever there is confusion the devil is always present.

- Have you ever sensed an attack from the devil on your life? What happened? How did you respond?

- Our fighting as Christians is seen in standing as Saints. In what ways do you stand for the Lord?

- The good news for the believer in Christ Jesus is this; we fight using God's strength, power, and might. God does not depend on you to fight alone; God is empowering you to fight knowing that He is with you!

A Short Talk With God

Jesus Christ, you are my Lord of Hosts! You are my God of battle and my victorious King. Thank you for empowering me to stand and to fight knowing that my fight is fixed because I win in the end. I praise you with this battle cry from my ready field of combat to your throne in eternal glory, HALLELUJAH! In my Lord's name, Jesus, I pray Amen!

Day 4-Week 6
The Truth About Grace

I was once asked to visit a home of a lady who was ill. I got the address and made my way to Beaumont's south end. When I arrived at the house there were no cars in the driveway, which I thought was odd. But, I was in a rush, so I just knocked on the door. I heard a voice say, "Just a minute!" A nice little old lady answered. I said, "I'm looking for one of my members from Antioch that needs prayer. She said, "We don't go to no church, but we do need some prayers. My daughter is in that bedroom and something done got a hold of her. She just won't come out of there. Will you pray for her?" Here is the total truth. Okay, I wanted to say, "I'm at the wrong house, and I'm not going in that room. Call the police and maybe they can help you." Are you feeling me?

I told this old lady I would be glad to pray. She said, "Okay, follow me." She started down this unlit hallway, and I was starting to think "Didn't I see this scene before on a horror film? Isn't this the point where people with common sense run?" When the woman got close to the door she said, "Open it." I almost said something completely unbecoming of a Christian, let alone a pastor. But I said, "Sure ma'am." I knocked on the door and said, "This is Pastor Adolph from Antioch Baptist Church. May I enter to have a word of prayer with you?" A kind voice said, "Yes, come in." I opened that door, and there sat a woman clearly demon possessed. When she saw me, she crawled up into a corner like an animal set to attack. The old woman said, "Yeah, something done got her" and walked off from me. I wanted to say, "Hey come back here and help me with this woman!"

As I walked slowly into the room, I noticed that the woman blinked uncontrollably and she laughed and grinned, as I got closer. All of a sudden calmness came over me. I walked to the bed and took her hand. It was cold. I started to pray. She was trying to get away from me but she couldn't. What was strange was I was barely holding her hand. It was the strength of the Lord. I commanded in a soft voice that any spirit that was in her that was not of God come out. The first time, the spirit within her laughed. I declared it again, and the woman laid down like a child prepared for a nap. It was as if she was tired and exhausted.

Here is the truth about grace, demonic forces are real. The great news of the day is God will give you His strength to fight spiritual battles. You do not need anything but His authority and His power because the devil is not our God's equal he is just our God's adversary. Our God has no equal, and when you stand in combat, you stand with His authority on your life.

The Treasure Of His Goodness

For we wrestle not against flesh and blood, but against principalities, against powers, against the rulers of the darkness of this world, against spiritual wickedness in high places (6:12, KJV).

1. First of all, notice the word "against" and how it is used. What Paul is doing is categorizing how demonic figures function.

2. "Principalities" are demons that attach themselves to people and families. Certain demons attach themselves to families, and you will have some things that just run in the family that need to be run off by the family. Then Paul mentions "powers." These are demonic attacks against systems. This is where the idea and reality of systemic evil come from. It has its roots in the fact that demons attack systems just like they do people. This is why no system filled with people is without some presence of demonism on earth.

3. Paul now mentions "rulers." These are demonic figures that attack leaders of every sort, especially those involved with government. This is why the Bible tells us to pray for our leaders (1 Tim. 2:1-3) because leaders are always under some spiritual attack.

4. Lastly, Paul brings to the forefront, "spiritual wickedness in high places." These are demons that patrol the earth's atmosphere. These beasts will be cast down when the Arch Angel Michael defeats them in Battle (Rev. 12:7-9).

5. The word "wrestle" in the Greek comes from the word *pale*. It was used by a soldier on the battlefield doing hand-to-hand combat. This is important because demonic attack does not always come from a distance. In most instances, it comes from proximity. This is why it is imperative that you choose carefully who you let near you.

The Triumph That He Gives

- Have you ever found yourself praying for your Pastor and did not know why? Has studying this passage helped you to understand why such prayers are essential?

- Take a close look at your family. Have you ever noticed specific moral ills or even certain physical illnesses that run from generation to generation? Are you aware that demonic figures could cause these issues?

- In what ways can you see demons in government?

- In what ways can you see demonic activity involved in systems and leadership?

- Have you ever seen the enemy attack you personally? What happened? Did it involve a person? What took place?

A Short Talk With God

Lord keep me day by day is my solemn supplication. I lift my family, my leaders, my pastor and other servants to you right now. Do for us what you have always done and be for us what you have always been, victory in the face of the enemy. In the name of our risen King, Jesus I pray, Amen!

Day 5-Week 6
The Truth About Grace

I love watching the game of football. On a Sunday afternoon, nothing makes me happier than to sit around after a beautiful day of worship, dinner with my family and gather around a boob-tube and check out men grapple on the gridiron. I love it! The speed, the strength, the muscle, the dogfights, and the combat make football an exciting sport! On one occasion, I made a mistake and turned on a Rugby game. It was a trip. It was the NFL, but with no pads.

You see, in the National Football League, you have to strap it on. You have to get dressed for battle. You cannot just show up at game time ready to play in socks and cleats. You have to have a helmet on your head, shoulder pads for your shoulders and upper back, a rib protector for the crushing blows you might receive to the mid-section, thigh pads, hip pads, knee pads, elbow pads, and gloves. It is gear needed for the game.

A Christian who shows up for spiritual battle without being dressed is just like a defensive end in the NFL showing without being padded down. You are not prepared without the proper gear.

Here is the truth about grace; God has given us the gear for the game that leads to our victory. Put it on and expect to win!

The Treasure Of His Goodness

Wherefore take unto you the whole armor of God, that ye may be able to withstand in the evil day, and having done all, to stand. Stand therefore, having your loins girt about with truth, and having on the breastplate of righteousness; and your feet shod with the preparation of the gospel of peace; above all, taking the shield of faith, wherewith ye shall be able to quench all the fiery darts of the wicked. And take the helmet of salvation, and the sword of the Spirit, which is the word of God: praying always with all prayer and supplication in the Spirit, and watching thereunto with all perseverance and supplication for all saints and for me, that utterance may be given unto me, that I may open my mouth boldly, to make known the mystery of the gospel, for which I am an ambassador in bonds: that therein I may speak boldly, as I ought to speak (6:13-20, KJV).

1. The armor of God consists of several pieces of equipment that are completely necessary for victory on the battlefield for our God.

2. First of all, there is the belt of truth. It holds up everything that a soldier has on as they fight. Secondly, the breastplate of righteousness is the cover that protects a soldier's upper torso. Here is the good news. Our righteousness is never ours; it is always righteousness that God gives us that belongs to Him. Next, there are cleats and they ensure the footing of a solider. On our feet is the Gospel of peace. This would be better put, the good news of the cross that brings us peace with God. In short, our sure found footing rests in the fact that Jesus Christ died, but early the third day morning on the Christian Sabbath, He rose from the grave with all power in His hands.

3. Next is the shield of faith. This shield is used to protect a soldier from the arrows that were lit that were shot by archers on the battlefield from a distance. In short, faith in God will keep you when you cannot see when the attacks are launched against you. Paul then mentions the helmet of salvation. This is the security in knowing where you stand with God eternally. And, lastly, there is the sword of the spirit, which is God's Holy Word. The word "sword" used here is the term **macharia**. It was a handheld sword with razor sharp blades that cut going and coming. It was designed to strike at a distance and provide the ultimate defensive weapon.

4. Notice that none of the weapons cover the back of a soldier only the front. This is because the job of other saints is to cover your back. Most importantly, Paul mentions "…. praying always…" A close study of this passage reveals that the real battle of a believer is standing. We are told to stand over and over and over again. The place of combat for the believer is praying. This is why we should pray always.

5. Spiritual combat is inevitable, but victory in Christ Jesus is achievable if we fight from a position and posture of prayer!

The Triumph That He Gives

-   Christians are commanded numerous times in this passage to stand. In what way do you feel believers have compromised this and have not taken a stand?

- Have you ever been hit and knocked down and you did not want to stand any longer? What happened to you?

- Spiritual combat is very real. Have you ever had to do spiritual battle in any way? What took place in your life?

- Prayer is the battleground for the believer in Jesus Christ. How has prayer empowered you as a Christian?

- The only way for a believer to make it is with other believers fighting alongside them. We cannot afford to fight each other. What can you do to help promote spiritual unity in the body of Christ so that we fight together and do not fall apart?

A Short Talk With God

Lord help me to stand. Empower me to stand. Strengthen me to stand. Lift me with your mighty hand so that I might stand. Thank you Jesus, this for the standing power you have given me. I have been hit, and I have been hurt, but my battle is not over and my fight to keep on standing continues. I bless you right now for the answered prayers of my past and the spiritual victories that have come my way because of you. I love you Jesus, and I owe you my all. In your precious and powerful name, I pray. Amen.

Day 6-Week 6
The Truth About Grace

Have you ever opened a letter and it brought you great joy? It happened to me while I was attending Morehouse School of Religion in Atlanta, Georgia. Previously, I had attended Texas Southern University and lived on campus. So I had the best of both worlds. I was from Houston and could go home when I wanted to, and I was a student on campus so I could disappear when it was necessary. Catch my drift?

When I moved to Atlanta, I had no such privileges any longer. I was twelve hours away from home, and I did not know a soul. It was a feeling I had never had before in my life. Yes, I was twenty-four years old and yes I was grown, but being that far away from home for me was crazy. I could not drive home and say hello to everyone right quick. I could not visit my parents' house and invade the kitchen like a wildebeest looking for leftovers. I was alone.

I was having a lonely moment and was thinking about transferring to Houston Baptist University. After all, seminary is just seminary, and I could help my father at his church. It would be the best of both worlds. Not to mention, I could move back into my three-bedroom, two-bathroom house that I had swapped for a dormitory room, community shower and campus life again. I was thinking about putting an end to the madness and going home.

I went downstairs to collect my bills and in my stack of payables was a letter with handwriting on it I readily recognized. It was from my momma! I opened it, and she had taken the time to write me. She told me how proud of me she was and to endure until the end. She said that she was sad to see me go, but happy to see me leave because God had great things in store for me. That one letter changed everything! Just hearing from someone who cared pushed me to the next level of growth and grace in the Lord Jesus Christ.

Here is the truth about grace, God knows what you need when you need it, and He will always provide it for you.

The Treasure Of His Goodness

But that ye also may know my affairs, and how I do, Tychicus, a beloved brother and faithful minister in the Lord, shall make known to you all things: whom I have sent unto you for the same purpose, that ye might know our affairs, and that he might comfort your hearts. Peace is to the brethren, and

love with faith, from God the Father and the Lord Jesus Christ. Grace be with all them that love our Lord Jesus Christ in sincerity. Amen (6:21-24, KJV).

1. The Apostle Paul wrote this letter to the Christians located in the Ephesus. It was one of Paul's churches that he had founded and just wanted to exhort, encourage and enlighten them in the faith.

2. Paul mentions a good servant whose name is Tychicus because he is a fellow laborer with Paul. The good news about this man is that he is nothing more than a servant. He does not wear any other title. This is an excellent lesson as the letter concludes. All too often, we are title happy when the truth is, titles are not as important as true servants are.

3. This letter ends with one word that by now I hope you know and appreciate. He concludes by saying, "Grace be with you…" Go back and look at day two-week one. Paul opens with grace and closes with grace. The reason for this is because grace was his reason for writing this marvelous letter.

4. The grace of this letter is the grace that I hope you desire and long to have.

5. It is a grace that I chose not to live without because if the grace of Ephesians is true I WANT SOME TOO!

Other Books and Articles by John R. Adolph

Books

I'm Changing the Game

Not Without A Fight

I'm Coming Out of This

Just Stick to the Script

Victorious Christian Living Volume I

Victorious Christian Living Volume II

Let Me Encourage You Volume I

Let Me Encourage You Volume II

The Him Book

Marriage Is For Losers

Celibacy is for Fools

Victory: Ten Fundamental Beliefs That Eradicate Defeat in the Life of a Christian

Articles-Zondervan Press

He Loves Me, He Loves Me, He Loves Me

I'm Certain That He Loves Me

His Love Made The Difference

God's Mind Is Made Up, He Loves You

To purchase additional copies of this book or other books published by Advantage Books call our order number at: 407-788-3110 (Book Orders Only) or visit our bookstore website at: www.advbookstore.com

Longwood, Florida, USA

"we bring dreams to life"™

www.advbookstore.com

CPSIA information can be obtained
at www.ICGtesting.com
Printed in the USA
LVHW082337291018
595298LV00020B/473/P